Prime Time:

Flourishing After 60

Diane S. Schaupp, Ph.D.

1st WORLD
PUBLISHING

Prime Time:

Flourishing After 60

Diane S. Schaupp, Ph.D.

© Diane S. Schaupp 2007

Published by 1stWorld Publishing
1100 North 4th St. Fairfield, Iowa 52556
tel: 641-209-5000 • fax: 641-209-3001
web: www.1stworldpublishing.com

First Edition

LCCN: 2007939504
SoftCover ISBN: 978-1-4218-9827-8
HardCover ISBN: 978-1-4218-9826-1
eBook ISBN: 978-1-4218-9828-5

This material has been written and published solely for educational purposes. The author and the publisher shall have neither liability or responsibility to any person or entity with respect to any loss, damage or injury caused or alleged to be caused directly or indirectly by the information contained in this book.

To my mother, Marion H. Pasqua,
and
To my mother-in-law, Betty Covington,
and
To my husband, Hugh.

TABLE OF CONTENTS

Part IV: The Life You Can Create

Reflections

Turning 60 is the autumn of life. The changing colors of life's autumn leaves are from the breezes of gentle winds (sometimes not so gentle) and the frosts endured along life's path. The beauty of the colors of life glisten in the sunlight of wisdom. As our youth is no longer, autumn can be reviewed on its own as a prime time of life.

Turning 60—the time when one's inner life is calmer, when the thoughts of ensuing winter prompt us to be forever grateful for life's harvests. Turning 60 has many rewards—the gentle support of friends from across the life-span remind us of who we are and where we've come, parents who have already seen winter and have shown us how to live comfortably in the snow, our children in the summer of life who are productive yet supportive in their warmth, and our grandchildren who are in the spring of life with tender buds and growth that unfolds as we nurture them.

D. S.

Acknowledgements

The emotional generosity of people throughout my life fills me with gratitude. I am grateful to many aging family members who helped prepare my aging self. They are as follows: my maternal grandparents, Anna and Harry Harrington; my maternal great aunt, Ethel Rees; my paternal great aunt and uncle, Effie and Allie Sill; my paternal aunt, Doris Buchenau; my mother, Marion Pasqua, and my mother-in-law, Bette Mae Covington.

In my 20s and 30s, I worked as a visiting nurse in New York City and New Jersey. This involved working daily with the challenges facing the then aging population. I spent hours listening to their stories. I am grateful to these aging adults who took me into their confidence and shared their stories with me.

Today, as I did in my 20s and 30s, I take note of those women and men who are in their 70s, 80s, and after to make sure I am not missing meaningful insights into aging. When I see my older patients, friends, and colleagues asking tough questions or offering meaningful insights, I see that none of those valuable qualities fade away; I am grateful for their wisdom.

I am grateful to a group of colleagues and friends who

wrote letters of support for my writing of *Prime Time* during the holiday season of 2005. They are: Dr. Lynn Mollick, Dr. Milton Spett, Dr. Andrea Green, Elizabeth Zack, Dr. Joseph Ganz, Wendy Meyer, Sandra Odian, Hannah Fox, Dr. Merle Keitel, Hugh R. Covington, Janie B. Schildge, Rosemarie McCabe, Dr. Lisa Piemont, Mary Lou Marcino, Linda Sugar, Dr. Gail Winbury, Marion Pasqua, Dr. Fiona Byrne, Dr. Elaine Pace, and Dr. Bernard Chelis. Thank you for your continuing support in helping me spread the word about *Prime Time*.

I am also very grateful to my husband for his unending support and plethora of ideas. And to Sandi Mann, whose patience in typing and retyping and getting copy to me punctually, has been a godsend. I am also appreciative for the literary skill, professionalism, and creativity of my original editor, Elizabeth Zack. I also want to thank Janice Pieroni for her wonderful mentoring on how to promote *Prime Time*.

The staff at 1st World Publishing deserve enormous credit. Ed Spinella, Evelyn Perricone, Leah Waller, and Rodney Charles were the final word on getting *Prime Time: Flourishing After 60* out to you the reader.

Finally, I want to thank you, the reader, for helping me spread the important word about how we can flourish after age 60 and dispel the negative stereotypes about aging.

Introduction

Have you created the life you wanted for yourself?

Are you the person you hoped to be?

What is left, now that youth has passed and the autumn of your life is beckoning? Is there a sense of fulfillment and continuing hope? Or does an aura of sadness and finality color everything, dimming your hopes, desires, and even your thoughts?

When I turned 60, the transition into later adulthood filled me with mixed feelings. I was grateful for the full life I had lived already: blessed with a soul-satisfying career; a loving husband, children, stepchildren, and a grandchild; rich and enduring friendships; and good health. Yet the idea of entering the autumn of life made me uneasy. Turning 60 brought home mortality and the finite nature of life.

I find that I'm not alone in my feelings. Many others dread "zero birthdays." In turning 60, we begin to become aware of physical and mental changes that are happening to us, making it more difficult to do many of the activities we once took for granted.

It takes longer to do things such as work tasks or

household chores. Increasingly, we find it harder to hear friends when listening to loud music. We forget simple things like phone numbers, and find words are more often just on the tip of our tongues. Sleeping at night can be fitful, making it helpful to replenish ourselves by sleeping late in the mornings. It becomes a struggle to get out of low chairs. Keys and reading glasses are misplaced often, and a glass or two of alcohol in the evening seems to have twice the potency that it did 20 years earlier.

These changes force us to wonder about our survival. We have thoughts about the finality of death, and of life as a finite commodity that cannot be replenished. Unlike money or material assets, time once spent is gone and irreplaceable. Often we begin to reconsider the meaning of the lives we've led, asking ourselves, "Who am I? Who am I *really*? And is this what I want out of life?"

Many people experience a midlife crisis, traditionally during their 40s. This crisis is often at a time when it is more possible to make major life changes than later in life. It is more possible at 45 than at 62 to make a career shift, to leave a marriage or enter into one, or to make geographic or total lifestyle changes. None of these changes are easy, but they are easier in the fourth or fifth decade of life.

At 60, though, questioning oneself and wanting to make changes is accompanied by an inner turmoil and conflict that is confounded by the acute awareness that the end of one's life is getting nearer and nearer. One is more mindful of one's frailty than ever, as what were once simply fears about one's survival now are more reality-based.

This inner turmoil and renewed interest in self-awareness and how one has lived life is typical of people as they reach their later years. It is common to look back and mourn earlier, pleasurable times of life. Although such tendencies have

Diane S. Schaupp, Ph.D.

been true of the past several generations, they are particularly relevant right now for the baby boomer generation, a group traditionally regarded as inspiring all kinds of societal changes.

The Influence of a Different Kind of Generation

I am of the first wave of baby boomers, the 75-million adults born from 1946 to 1964 who started turning 60 starting in 2006.

Like many others who are part of the first generation of baby boomers, I was raised in the overwhelming presence of television and advertising. We were the first generation to observe different lifestyles through television. This media exposed us to many injustices, including race, prejudice, and war. As a result, in the 1960s the boomers became involved in doing what they could to change perceived societal injustices.

As many of us entered adulthood during the 1970s, we found ourselves grappling with the uncertainties of establishing our own personal values and a mature sense of identity distinct from that of our parents. We realized that although it was difficult to change the world, we could at least change ourselves. Thus, a new market of introspective self-help books emerged.

As is common in the fourth decade of life, we began moving up the economic ladder and pursuing more materialistic goals. The "hippies" of the 1960s became the "yuppies" of the 1980s. We married and became parents, realizing that many roles and rules of our parents and families no longer worked for our generation. Dual-income couples became commonplace; so did divorce. Society institutionalized those changes, in the form of day care centers, after-school care, family therapy, and joint custody.

The boomers, who transformed marriage and childbirth by demanding to be informed and have their needs met, were also involved in creating change in terms of how women viewed and moved through menopause. Instead of bolstering the misconception that menopause is horrible for women, boomers found that the end of their reproductive years marked the beginning of a new time of life—one of sexual vitality and freedom.

Without a doubt, baby boomers have intensified the experience of whatever they are encountering at each moment of their lives. It seems that when they reach any stage of life, their issues dominate the social and political themes of the time. Simply put: They do things differently than the way things were done before.

Because of their historical context, questioning attitude, and level of consciousness, they are more accepting of change and diversity. Now that the children of the 1960s *are* 60, many, myself included, are challenging the culture's limited, one-sided view of aging as a period of inevitable decline, significant chronic illness, and loss of meaningful roles. They are reinventing the notion of retirement, and what it means to live with maturity, wisdom, and fulfillment in the later half of life. They want to find pleasure in the present, and to eagerly anticipate the future.

Change is a Way of Life

As a counseling psychologist, I have spent years helping people adjust as they pass through the various psychological developmental phases of the life cycle. I know that in the later years, although there are a number of losses we come to experience, we can, as aging adults, keep the scales tipped toward the positive side with the right attitude, thoughtful inward reflection, and awareness and appreciation of our interconnectedness to all of life.

Turning 60, after all, means that entering the autumn of life can be viewed on its own as a time of magnificent beauty; at the same time, autumn is a period to reflect on the ensuing winter of life. Yes, there will probably be evidence of decline with accompanying aches and pains. But at the same time, turning 60 is a time when one has the chance to further develop one's inner beauty and wisdom. The thoughtful and rewarding changes that can be made to one's inner life allow one to fully embrace the often-elusive quality of learning how to take pleasure in the present—instead of honoring only the past—and live the remainder of one's life to the fullest. This time of life can be viewed as "the prime of life" if this art of mastering pleasure in the moment is achieved.

Personally and professionally, I fully recognize that in understanding and working through the inevitable changes we encounter as we age, as well as the changes in other areas we need or want for ourselves, our future will be as bright…as *we make it.*

A New and Profound Sense of Self

This book provides us with a new sense of self—one that lives deeply and authentically in the universe, one that does not struggle to cling to a youth-oriented culture when one's physical body is moving into a different time of year.

As mature, thoughtful adults, we can recognize the physical diminishments of aging while drawing on inner resources that contribute to our personal fulfillment and wisdom. Not only will this book help us understand who we are and how we arrived where we are, but it will empower us to be the people we want to be. It will give us more control over the ways in which we lead the remainder of our lives so that we can continue to move towards peace and fulfillment and master the art of finding pleasure in the present.

This may sound like a huge promise. It's not. Every day boomers are finding that by getting to know their inner selves better, they are creating a richer life despite life's various challenges. Honest self-reflection is the beginning of an important part of one's psychological development, and it can make the later years of life rich and meaningful experiences. We can live out the last third of our lives fully satisfied with who we are as we age, if only we are ready to make some changes...both those that are inevitable and those over which we have some control.

> For those of you who are concerned about your financial security, the ideas in this book might seem a bit lofty. Your life may be enriched by spending a short time each day integrating some of the ideas into your life.

Diane S. Schaupp, Ph.D.

PART I

AGELESS BEAUTY

Chapter I

A New Vision

From the moment we are born, we are on a journey. We move through life in cycles of beginnings and endings, experiencing new ventures, changing as we go. Throughout time, human beings have recognized this need to change and develop through life's journeys.

Many indigenous communities look to a spirit greater then themselves for direction as they journey through life. The Chinese speak of Tao as "the way," the path of the Tao is revealed by looking at the patterns of life as they unfold. The Bible, too, is full of metaphors that describe journeys, from the Israelites journeying out of Egypt to the Promised Land, to the themes of hopefulness found in the cycle of loss and rebirth.

Most journeys involve both leaving and returning. Later life is a time of returning, full of experience, lessons learned, and gifts to give. It is a time of coming home, a time to look within and make sense of our lives.

Carl Jung suggested that our life's journey first starts with its morning, the time of youth and first maturity. During this time, most of us devote our time to the conventional concerns of establishing ourselves in the world, marrying, and having children. Yet when the afternoon of life arrives, we can no longer live by morning's program. We need to start to turn inward, to reconnect with aspects of ourselves that we silenced or failed to heed in our efforts to create social identities and develop careers.[1]

Yet many of us never take this path, choosing instead to maintain our focus on the concerns of morning. As Betty Friedan notes, many of us "have barely ever considered the possibilities of Age for new kinds of loving intimacy, purposeful work and activity, learning and knowing, community and care....For to see age as continual human development involves a revolutionary paradigm shift."[2] Instead of perceiving that aging's journey involves growth and incredible possibilities, we have been prone to see it in an entirely different light, one limited by time and circumstance.

Why We Think the Way We Do About Getting Older

A negative perspective on age and what it means to be "old" took hold of America during the Industrial Revolution. Throughout history, elders had always assumed honored positions in society, revered as gurus, shamans, wise women, and wise men who guided society and taught the mysteries of the human spirit. Part of the worth ascribed to age arose from the fact that economic worth was linked to the value of family property, with the ownership of such land most often resting in the hands of parents and grandparents.

But, technology seemed to change the way America viewed aging. New ways of business, with which America's elders were unfamiliar, took a stronghold on the economy and the American mind-set. Youthful energy and mobility became prized over experience and wisdom, and new, city-based occupations offered the younger generation social

Diane S. Schaupp, Ph.D.

and financial freedom. The shapers of society became its burdens, and the youth culture became dominant.

The adoration of youth continued as the years passed, and we came to fear growing old. While in his 50s, Daniel Levinson gloomily confirmed in *Seasons of a Man's Life* that a man approaching 60 "fears that the youth within him is dying and that only the old man, an empty, dry structure devoid of energy and foolish old age yet remain."[3] Author Bernice Neugarten succinctly noted that "we [Americans] find the prospect of old age particularly unattractive."[4]

Fortunately, the thinking about aging as a process of inevitable decay took on shades of gray, and became no longer so black and white. Robert Butler and Herbert P. Gleason captured the conflict in perspective in 1981, commenting that "from the *biological* [emphasis mine] perspective, aging is a predictable, progressive, universal deterioration of various physiological systems, mental and physical, behavioral and biomedical....At the same time, there is clear evidence, though more elusive and more difficult to measure, of concurrent psychosocial growth [emphasis missing] in capabilities for strategy, sagacity, prudence, wisdom [in age]."[5]

Betty Friedan, in summarizing the findings of the research on aging, pointed out that "the decline in various capabilities with age...has turned out not to be universal and predictable, as it would be if it were biologically programmed."[6] It started becoming clear that after 60, the strength of our capabilities seemed to depend less on biology and more on our particular environments, changes in society, and individual choices and patterns of living.

In this way, the minds of many Americans slowly began to awaken to the possibility that, if they put their minds to it, they could capture, and be the reflection of, what is now viewed as "successful aging."

Aging Successfully

More and more scientific studies began to reveal that we could eat for longevity by choosing antioxidant-rich foods that provide nutrition and defense against disease, and that we could counteract the effects of a slowing metabolism and keep our bones healthy by thoughtful exercise.

But, the emphasis was not all on the physical. An active life was viewed as essential to combat physical and intellectual decline, with social activities recognized as being able to "maintain health by stimulating more physical and mental activity, by provoking a social network...and by maintaining a sense of self-esteem and social worth."[7]

We began to stimulate our aging minds with travel plans, social engagements, and exciting hobbies. Many baby boomers seen in my private practice and others I know personally plan to work well into their 70s for both financial and self-fulfilling reasons.

Yet what is it that lies behind the drive to be perceived as aging "successfully"? If we dig just a little beneath the surface, many of us can come to see that much of what motivates our actions is not necessarily our willingness to accept the fact that we are growing older, but a denial of aging, and the obstinate refusal to recognize any symptoms of mental or physical deterioration.

Thomas Cole gives voice to this inner and often unconscious strategy in *The Journey of Life*. He points out that "the one-sided drive to alter, reverse, or somehow control the biological process of aging actually impoverishes its meaning. So-called positive aspects of aging turn out to be disguised efforts to restore youth rather than attempts to appreciate growing old as a fundamental part of human existence."[8] Our choice to erase our wrinkles with plastic surgery often is

Diane S. Schaupp, Ph.D.

part of a refusal to accept the fact that as the days pass, we are growing older, and that being older isn't so bad. Even those aging adults with high levels of self-esteem struggle with age discrimination, especially in work environments, despite changes in a positive direction. Attitudes are always behind legislation.

By trying to look and "be" young, we uphold the illusion that we are both ageless and immortal. We fail to recognize that the afternoon of life holds a special and unique importance for every one of us.

Keys to a Successful Life Journey

Jung writes, "A human being would certainly not grow to be seventy or eighty years old if this longevity had no meaning for the species. The afternoon of human life must also have a significance of its own and cannot be merely a pitiful appendage to life's morning." In fact, Jung went so far as to suggest, "Whoever carries over in the afternoon the law of the morning…must pay for it with damage to the soul…."[9]

At such a point in our lives, we find that we do have life experiences that inform our decision-making process and our capacity to influence others in a positive way. And Betty Friedan, after extensively reviewing the research on aging, clarifies that the "accurate, realistic, active identification with one's own aging—as opposed both to resignation to the stereotype of being 'old' and denial of age changes—seem an important key to vital aging, and even longevity."[10]

To continue a vital involvement in life, we must accept age-related changes, and respond to life and its changing circumstances with *personal adaptability*. This means having and creating goals until the end of life, whether it is modifying our goals to fit the needs of the age we have become, or finding entirely new ones for ourselves as we experience the aging journey. Yet doing so requires that we embrace change…and that, of course, can be unsettling. As a matter of course, later life itself demands almost continual changes on our part as we move into its constantly evolving series of interwoven cycles, each with their own unique problems, challenges, and dreams.

A Cyclical Life

The cycles of aging that soon will be described can serve as a framework for examining your life journey.

As you read the material that follows, start thinking about your life. What do you want from life on a "go-forward" basis? What have you learned? And what do you need to do now to make the rest of your life enjoyable and meaningful? Before you do so, confirm with yourself that you *want* this new sense of self, a sense of self that lives deeply and authentically in the universe; a sense of self that does not struggle to cling to the youth-oriented culture when in reality the body is moving into a new season or time of day.

Do you want to be a "later" adult (a term used in this book for those in the later third of life) who recognizes the physical diminishments of aging while at the same time draws on inner resources that contribute to the development of wisdom? If your answer is "yes," or even a "maybe," you are sure to continue on the complex but intriguing developmental journey that is your life, and come to the recognition that you are not only who you are today, but an accumulation of all that you have been before.

Diane S. Schaupp, Ph.D.

The Autumn of Life

The arrival at later life—which I identify in this book as the point at which we turn 60—can be both miserable and joyous, depending on what our personal assessment of our lives proves to be and how we react to the changes that start to affect our lives. Simply put, turning 60 calls for important self-reflection, and our reactions to such things as change, disease, and conflict contribute to how we age, and how quickly we do so.

During this time period we move into three psychological stages that typify the aging process. However, these stages are not static; we can move fluidly back and forth through the stages as we address the challenges of each, or not. These stages are:

+ later adulthood, from age 60 to 75;

+ early elderhood, from age 76 to 95; and

+ later elderhood, from age 96 and beyond.

Later Adulthood

During this time of life we start to reconsider the burning question "Who *am* I?" and engage in repeated soul searching. We examine our lives by reviewing past accomplishments, reconciling our past expectations with our present reality and our future goals. We closely consider our choices, whether they were to follow a particular career path or a call of the heart, as well as the individual answers we received, to come to terms with what is valuable to, and honored by us, as individuals.

Such intimate, inward reflection may make this period a tumultuous time. Many dwell negatively on the past and their actions, to the point that they allow the negative feelings of the past to take precedence over current circumstances. New events are then unable to compete with past memories in terms of engaging their attention, and many become depressed, thinking always of "what could have been."

Some people's inward search leads them to become self-confident to an extreme. To protect the image they hold of themselves, they see their own lives as models for younger people, and are unable to tolerate any implications of having failed at some point along their desired path. They reject all old doubts about themselves, and present a portrait of total self-confidence to those around them. In becoming inflexible about their beliefs, these individuals are viewed by others as lacking in compassion and empathy.

Some, however, respond to such internal examinations of the past by attaining a new, positive level of self-acceptance. When we learn to know ourselves—for better or for worse—and remain as objective as possible about our lives when we look back, it allows for the formation of a confident self-image so that we can embrace the future and its changes, become personally adaptable, and treat others with compassion and empathy. We look back on our lives and recognize moments of truth and bravery, and moments of self-deception and cowardice. We come to acknowledge the decisions that made our lives worth living, as well as the choices that adversely affected our lives. We take the time to appreciate the people who benefited us, who affected our lives and helped us become who we are today, and we can even come to see our enemies in new ways, determining what led us into conflict or to a change we made in our lives because of it.

Diane S. Schaupp, Ph.D.

Growing as a Couple

Nancy and Bob, ages 64 and 62, have been married for over 30 years. Both are professionals. They are thrilled that their family financial responsibilities are ending: one of their young adult children is married, the other is engaged, and the third has just graduated with an advanced degree. For the first time in many years, they are free of educational costs.

Both Nancy and Bob are experiencing the turmoil of later adulthood as they sort out their options. Bob feels he is ready for early retirement: he changed jobs a few years ago because he wanted to be nearer Nancy, who had taken an excellent career offer several states away that put her closer to her surviving mother and two of their three children. Bob had spent 25 years at his previous company, and he docs not feel as committed to his new employer. He wants to spend more time with his wife and enjoy the beauty of the home they bought. Nancy is not sure whether she is ready to retire, as she had taken time off from her career years ago when the children were young.

As the couple discuss their options and examine their past, they are able to accept the different roles each of them want to play at this point in their lives. Bob is able to forgive himself for not feeling up to meeting all the challenges at his new job, as he had 25 productive and successful years at his prior company. In turn, while Nancy wants to remain at her new job, she is able to admit to being tired of having to lead large numbers of employees. Both are able to take pride in their professional accomplishments even when those accomplishments sometimes fell short of their expectations, and now choose to follow the path that will bring them closest to inner contentment, even though the path is different for each of them.

Author Norbert Glas discusses what is needed in the self-examination process in his book, *Fulfillment of Old Age*:

> You are now on the point of entering a period during which strange things will be happening to you. Perhaps you may feel that everything in your life is drawing to a close, and because the present does not succeed in satisfying you, you may feel the urge to return to your past. You will be inclined to cling to memory pictures that have remained within you from the past, and these may now well up in you with more force than ever. Many past things will take on a golden hue. But you must not allow yourself to be depressed by the gentle sadness of self-pity because of what you have lost and is now no more. This would be of no help to you, and would indeed hinder you from achieving a worth-while old age. You ought indeed to examine your past carefully, but only for the purpose of understanding the true reasons for events. Do not lose yourself in sentimental reveries. This would not lend you support any more than indulging in regrets for what you have lost. Only complete sincerity in your self-examination can help you.[11]

Yet this stage of life is not only about *internal* self-examination, as aging brings with it unique internal, external, and intellectual changes.

The Challenges

First, we must work through the problems and issues of a changing body. We find our sexual needs change, moving from a hormonally driven sexuality to one more dependent on intimacy and loving kindness. Some of us encounter declining health, beset by chronic illness or daily but constant

Diane S. Schaupp, Ph.D.

aches and pains. Many of us find it difficult to deal with moving more slowly and carefully through life.

Second, we must wrestle with a perceived loss of power and responsibility that arises from the sometimes necessary decision to move to a retirement and/or smaller home. The decision may be for the best rationally, but emotionally, it can be a decision that tugs at the heart, while intellectually it is often a choice that demands we set aside unhelpful pride.

Third, although in many Eastern cultures later adulthood is regarded as a period when people are freed from the challenges of everyday life and may spend their time working out their relationship to God and the Universe, in Western cultures most become more focused on activities to engage the bodies and minds rather than on contemplation and how to live with where they are now. The challenge is to strike a balance which pleases and satisfies us.

Fourth, our relationships start to change—in stark, dramatic ways. At this stage we frequently begin to face the loss of friends, partners, and quite possibly the children who should have been immortal and who represent the best parts of us. Their deaths provide us with huge sources of psychological stress. We grapple with grief as we mourn, and experience difficulty in coming to terms with the loss of companionship and of someone with whom we shared a world of memories and future plans. Moreover, if we watch those around us suffer long illnesses, or experience abrupt death in the midst of thriving and vigorous lives, we wonder about the value of life, including the value of our own.

The very notion of death causes quite an intellectual strain as we attempt to accept and/or understand these losses as well as our individual mortality. Many of us fear death, whether it be the fear related to the actual process of dying, what happens upon death, or both.

Lastly, in later adulthood, we begin having to come to terms with the negative stereotypes about aging that society puts forth, with its emphasis on youthful beauty and makeovers that keep us from looking our age. This traditionally has caused fear of aging, and negative or hostile attitudes between the different age groups.

This hurts all members of society—not just the old. When the elderly no longer can bring us in touch with our own aging, we generally start playing dangerous power games to uphold the illusion of being ageless and immortal. Then, not only does the wisdom of the elderly remain hidden, but the elderly themselves lose their own deepest understanding of life! The challenge is to overcome the negative stereotypes of aging and embrace the gifts of aging: self-acceptance, wisdom, and developing a point of view about death and our interdependence to all living beings.

Yet, if we become the ones who embody later life, how do we become so gracefully and honestly? By resolving our earlier developmental crises, such as learning to trust ourselves and others. By accepting our failures. By reclaiming our forgotten selves. By learning new dreams or revising long-held ones. By becoming gracefully aware of our vulnerabilities.

Unfortunately, some people are unable psychologically to move beyond the stage of later adulthood. They struggle continually with uneasiness about who they are and where they are at this stage of life. They come to dwell obsessively on past discouragements and disappointments, and eventually view their own frailties and vulnerabilities with scorn.

Others, though, positively resolve the challenges they face by integrating yesterday's memorable events and rough times with who they are today. This results in authenticity, wholeness, and soundness. Making sense of our lives leads to a wisdom in which the interconnectedness in all aspects of the

Diane S. Schaupp, Ph.D.

universe is understood.

Yet, most of us experience *both ends* of the continuum, positive and negative, as we resolve the psychological tasks of later adulthood. We mesh our authenticity with a discomfort over our acknowledged vulnerabilities. The experience of some negative resolution fosters or inspires our compassion, and an adaptive understanding of our own limitations.

Early Elderhood

In the early elderhood stage, there is a unique appreciation for change. Here we must cope with the physical changes of aging, knowing that a key to understanding and making any life decisions rests with recognizing our health status for what it is. Still, as chronic conditions begin to accumulate, they create difficulties when it comes to engaging in high levels of physical activity, social interaction, and independence.

We can experience "age-related slowing." We notice this on tasks and chores requiring mental processing: We find it difficult to go grocery shopping with only a mental list, for example, or remember a list of chores—getting gas, stopping at the dry cleaners, buying a birthday card and a gallon of milk—without writing them down first.

Many of us now have to confront critical decisions in terms of living arrangements. Many choose to change their living arrangements, downsizing their current living space because of physical ailments and limitations. Or, they seek a different home because they have lost a lifetime companion or because lifelong friends and neighbors have moved on or passed away. Still others make this decision because they want to follow a simpler lifestyle now that the children have moved away and are settled elsewhere, or because a change in their homes will provide them with more recreational opportunities and/or a climate more conducive to this stage of life. Sometimes it is financial difficulties that provide the impetus to move to a different locale. And yet, some early elders emphatically want to stay in their long-time residences.

Knowing What Is Right for You

Mary, 85 years old, has lived alone since her husband died 20 years ago. She maintains close contact via telephone with her daughters, both of whom—along with her grandchildren—live at least four hours away. Mary has many friends, is president of a social club; sings in her church choir, and writes poetry. Although she has a close male companion whom she met a few years after her husband died, they have decided that despite their commitment to each other, they will not marry, preferring to remain in their own homes so they don't have to go through "all the adjustments of marriage and living together."

Even when Mary fell recently and went to one of her daughters' homes to recuperate, she was anxious to return to her familiar surroundings. Mary explains, "When I am home, I feel independent and in control." Her daughters support her decision despite the fact that they worry about their mother's frailty and her current living situation. They recognize that Mary will probably remain far healthier psychologically in a familiar setting and neighborhood than in a retirement community closer to one of them.

As men and women age in this cycle, there is a blending of traditional gender roles, often because of advanced maturity, changes in hormone production, retirement; in

Diane S. Schaupp, Ph.D.

addition, women are more apt to outlive the men who have been their partners. In this stage, men become more willing to accept the help of others and prefer to spend more time at home, while women are more likely to pursue activities outside the home. They also are more apt to do simple tasks traditionally completed by the men in their lives: taking out the garbage, getting home repairs done, or traveling alone. Author Simone de Beauvoir has described how the elders of Bali embrace multidimensional gender roles, commenting, "The old have a very important role—both male and female —for the distinction between the sexes disappears with age. Their opinion is asked on every subject."[12]

And many find that despite the limitations and changes arising at this time of life, early elderhood often proves a creative and productive time, with many drawing, designing, writing, or exploring other personal interests.

Impressive at 76 and Beyond[13]

✝ At 80, George Burns won an Academy Award for his performance in The Sunshine Boys.

✝ At 81, Johann Wolfang von Goethe finished Faust.

✝ At 85, Coco Chanel was the head of a fashion design firm.

✝ At 88, Konrad Adenauer was chancellor of Germany.

✝ At 89, Arthur Rubinstein gave one of his greatest recitals at Carnegie Hall in New York City.

✝ At 89, Albert Schweitzer was the head of a hospital in Africa.

✝ At 91, Dr. Norman Vincent Peale was one of America's most sought-after speakers.

✝ At 91, Eamon de Valera was president of Ireland.

✝ 94, Bertrand Russell was active in international peace drives.

In terms of psychological development, most individuals in early elderhood have developed a point of view about death and confronted their fears. They now experience personal dignity about the choices they have made and the goals they have achieved over the years, no longer feeling despair over past failures, misfortunes, or missed opportunities.

However, conflict arises because early elders want to find a way to be remembered after their death. Most often they resolve this internal struggle by acknowledging the continuity of life and giving back to those in their families and communities. They choose to act as mentors who teach the young; as mediators who resolve civil, social, and intergenerational conflict; as monitors of public bodies such as city hall and Congress; as mobilizers of social change; and/or as motivators who urge people away from self-interest and toward the public good. Staying involved in the network of social relationships that arise from these roles allows them to feel immensely valued.

Later Elderhood

Psychologist and best-selling author, Mary Pipher, best describes those who achieve this stage of life in her book *Another Country*:

All have interests and relationships that sustain them. They have learned about psychological survival from their long and complicated lives. They aren't bitter or sulky; they are appreciative and grateful for a call from a friend, a sighting of a new bird or a good home-cooked meal. They find joy in small moments. They have mostly happy moments and balance the sorrows with humor....Most assume responsibility for their own choices. They are hard workers with a tremendous

Diane S. Schaupp, Ph.D.

sense of pride and accomplishment.[14]

When these elders reach the later stages of life, they have already seen great suffering, in terms of their own losses and of those around them; their response is compassion, rather than anger or sadness. Mary Pipher observes, "Later elders have strong spiritual beliefs. They believe in something larger that transcends their own egos."[15]

In addition, the historical perspective they have gained allows them to understand the place of change in a person's life. They know that change is a basic element of life, at both the level of the individual and the greater community. They realize that change's nature is cyclical, and also that change can bring about real progress.

As they are likely now to be parents, grandparents, and/or great-grandparents, they see that several generations of offspring brings a new degree of continuity to life. Their memories encompass their own grandparents as well as observations of their great-grandchildren. The insights gained from observing change and continuity are often passed on to the younger generations, and reflected in their current creative pursuits.

One of the greatest psychological challenges that remains in this stage is learning to accept personal vulnerability and to ask for help, something that can prove especially difficult after having been raised in a society of independence, youth orientation, and individuality. Indeed, many insist before becoming ill or frail that becoming independent is a sign of progress in life, and the need to lean on others a sign of weakness or indication of decline. It takes the greatest of courage to accept the inevitable dependency that comes with the physical limitations at this stage.

Psychologically, conflict arises around issues of loneliness. Some become especially lonely after they reject the help of others because of the shame they associate with being dependent on others. In addition, physical problems may interfere with their activities and keep them from coming into frequent contact with friends and acquaintances.

In addition, death robs them of cherished friends, and it becomes progressively more difficult to invest one's heart into new friendships. Yet those who stay distant and closed off find that their spirit for life dwindles, along with their physical powers.

103 and Still Enjoying Life...

Joe used to be the CEO of a billion-dollar corporation; now, at 103, he retains his positive attitude about his quality of life despite increasing physical limitations. He knew it was important to adapt to his changing physical competencies, so rather than try to maintain his corporate position at the top, he chose to be active in his son's business in a lesser position upon retirement. Since his wife died over 25 years ago, Joe lives on his own with a housekeeper (his children, grandchildren, and great-grandchildren all live close by). Physically, Joe has experienced decline, so he has used his financial resources to obtain medical devices such as a state-of-the-art hearing aid, pacemaker, arch supports, and a cane to help compensate for the physical limitations of aging. Joe keeps his attitude positive as he actively pursues his chosen hobbies, particularly in giving financially and personally to the community, to schools, and to charitable organizations.

Diane S. Schaupp, Ph.D.

Many studies have shown that elderly people with strong connections to at least one other person live longer and are more resilient to injury, illness, and emotional loss than people who are isolated. In an article in *Health Magazine* (September 1996) on longevity in Okinawa, socializing was found to be as important as diet: "Socializing is good for the body as well as for the soul."[16]

This stage of life therefore comes to redefine such things as kindness and courage: "To be kind is to accept help from the young,"[17] for example. There is no longer complete independence, but interdependency and mutuality. As Wendy Lustbader observes, "You [late elders] need us now, but we needed you when we were children. Our children need you now. We need each other. We are helping you because of respect and gratitude."[18]

And, in fact, *social support* is what contributes significantly to late elders' health and well-being. It helps reduce their sense of isolation, and when late elders have intimate companions in later life, they have a higher level of life satisfaction, feel valued, and in turn valuable. Further, the presence of caring family members provides a flow of critical resources including affection, information, advice, transportation, assistance with meals and daily activities, finances, and health care. The expectation that we will be able to count on kindness in time of need becomes one of our most sustaining beliefs, says Wendy Lustbader in *Counting on Kindness.*[19]

A New Dawn

It's clear that the process of aging, in all of its cycles, is one that presents itself with a number of unique challenges, all of varying difficulties. Yet we can accept and embrace them, and uncover the best outcome for us, although our successful response is very dependent on who we are, how we view ourselves, and how we embrace change.

To discover who you are right now, as well as who you have been across your life span, turn to the next chapter, "A Time for Self-Reflection."

Endnotes

1. C. G. Jung, "The Stages of Life," in J. Campbell, ed., *The Portable Jung* (New York: Viking, 1971), p. 12.

2. Betty Friedan, *The Fountain of Age* (New York: Simon & Schuster, 1993), pp. 75–82.

3. Daniel Levinson, *Seasons of a Man's Life* (New York: Knopf, 1978), p. ix.

4. Bernice Neugarten, *Middle Age and Aging* (Chicago and London: The University Press, 1968).

5. Robert N. Butler and Herbert P. Gleason, eds., *Productive Aging* (New York: Springer-Verlag, 1985), p. 7.

6. Betty Friedan, pp. 75–82.

7. Betty Friedan, pp. 75–82.

8. Thomas Cole, *The Journey of Life: A Cultural History of Aging in America* (New York: Cambridge University Press, 1992).

9. Carl G. Jung, p. 12.

10. Betty Friedan, p. 82.

11. Norbert Glas, *Fulfillment of Old Age* (New York: Steiner Books, 1987).

12. Simone de Beauvoir, *The Coming of Age* (New York: G. P. Putman, 1972), p. 76.

Diane S. Schaupp, Ph.D.

13. David Wallechinsky, Irving Wallace, and Amy Wallace, *The Book of Lists* (New York: William Morrow, 1977).

14. Mary Pipher, *Another Country: Navigating the Emotional Terrain of our Elders* (New York: Riverhead Books, 1999), pp. 241–245.

15. Mary Pipher, pp. 241–245.

16. Deborah Franklin, "The Healthiest Women in the World," *Health* (September 1996): 57–64.

17. Mary Pipher, pp. 241–245.

18. Wendy Lustbader, *Counting on Kindness* (New York: The Free Press, 1994), p. 75.

19. Wendy Lustbader, p. 75.

Chapter 2

A Time for Self-Reflection

The quest for meaning moves to the forefront of our lives in later years. Few of us were properly prepared for many of the obstacles in the road of life, and we learned the hard way that life doesn't always turn out as we envisioned when we were much younger.

As we encountered and took increasingly unexpected directions, many of us moved without looking back and understanding or integrating what had happened. Sometimes, the obstacles changed what we became. Other times, in an attempt to preserve ourselves and what we assumed was important, we responded on autopilot, and never thought to undo habits and change the patterns of our life. Yet the opportunity to do so is ours—at any point in our life.

We are born into a physical body with a skeletal structure, muscles, organs, hormones, senses, and a nervous system. We are received into a family with complex interrelation-ships—sister, brother, mother, father, perhaps. By being born to a particular set of parents in a particular place, certain things were given to us, such as gender, nationality, race, and physical constitution. But, as we develop through the life stages, we are given an opportunity to transform our personality and how we choose to live. *Reflection* is a useful process that allows us to investigate larger patterns in our life that we want to change.

Yet, it is hard to turn our attention within. Old habits and set patterns seem to dominate us easily. Although they may bring us suffering, we tend to accept them with almost fatalistic resignation. We are used to giving in to them. We may want freedom, but when it comes to our habits, we are completely enslaved.

Self-reflection can slowly bring wisdom—the wisdom to see we are behaving again and again in fixed, repetitive patterns. We may long to get out of them. We may, but then of course we may fall back into them, again and again. With reflection, however, we can slowly emerge from them and change. At age 60, when the autumn of life is upon us, many of us start to want to delve into ourselves in our search for truth, answers, pathways.

The Spirit of Change

Isn't everything always changing: the color of the leaves on the trees in the park, the light in your room, the seasons, the weather, the time of day? What about us? Doesn't everything we have done in the past seem like a dream now? The friends we grew up with, the childhood haunts, those views and opinions we once held with a single-minded passion—we have left them behind.

Look at a thought: it comes, it stays, and it goes. The past is history, the future is a great mystery, yet this moment is a gift—"that is why it is called a present." The only thing we really have is now.

Through self-reflection, one is able to make a real change in the depths of the heart, and to learn how to avoid the "pitfalls in life" and how to "move more gracefully though life." Often this requires deep contemplation, because only then can we truly open our eyes to what we are doing with our lives.

As we reflect, and go on reflecting, our hearts and minds go through a gradual transformation. We start letting go of things that were once important to us, and this process begins to feel more natural, becoming easier and easier. The more we develop a view of letting go, the more a shift takes place in our way of looking at everything.

A different energy goes into self-reflection now, and we come to possess a deeper understanding of how we have lived. There's a gathering of all the parts, as we work to knit them together consciously. We embrace all that we have lived, letting go of old grudges against ourselves and others. If we're open to it, we begin to see patterns that we reasoned away previously.

As changes occur, we learn to look at them with a new understanding. Then, something in us will shift, something will be different. The whole situation will now be more relaxed, less intense and painful. With each successive change, we realize a little bit more, and our view of living becomes deeper and more spacious.

When Nancy, first profiled in Chapter 1, reflected on her life, she recognized that what she learned in the 1960s about women's changing roles were half-truths. She vowed she would tell her grandchildren that the consciousness-raising of the 1960s did not effectively redefine women's roles: Nancy thought women still struggled with balancing the "yin and yang" in their lives.

As Nancy worked on rewriting her life story, the patterns and meanings of her life's journey started to be revealed. She says, for example, that no one had ever suspected she wasn't happy. Nancy recognized she was not asking herself if the activities consuming her life were bringing her happiness or if she was continuing to react to the expectations of others.

To fully understand herself, Nancy reflected on why she had made the choices she did. Nancy realized that she had the ability to tackle very difficult professional challenges and to be successful, even to win some acclaim for her accomplishments. But, she also realized that during her 50s her goals had changed. She had made it to the "top" rung of her career ladder. Now, she wanted more personal, rather than professional, satisfaction. She asked herself what she needed to change to pursue more personal happiness.

Diane S. Schaupp, Ph.D.

After self-reflection, Nancy decided she wanted to simplify her life. She took a job in a beautiful area near the ocean which she loves, and closer to her aging mother and children. As Nancy and Bob spoke of Nancy's relocation to accommodate her new job, Bob had originally planned to remain in their home while they decided if Nancy's move was a good one. Instead, once Bob put out his availability to his professional network, he entertained two lucrative job offers within two months of when Nancy had moved. Suddenly, Nancy's shift involved much larger life changes than she had imagined—clearing out all the collections of 30 years of marriage and three children, selling her home of 20 years, searching for a new home in a very expensive market, and tackling a new job in an unfamiliar culture without all of her previous professional networks. It was through the unraveling of each of these specific challenges that Nancy grew.

In reflecting on what she needed to do to pursue more personal happiness, Nancy found that what she had chosen turned out to be much different from what she had expected—much more challenging. But once the challenges were met, i.e., decision to retire, to reunite with her husband on a daily rather than a weekend basis, to travel more, to choose activities in which to be passionately involved rather than grudgingly obligated, to write more, to nurture life-affirming women friends, to eat better, and to exercise every day (hiking, biking, swimming, or yoga), she attained a calm and a peace that she had not allowed herself to experience in years. In two years, she felt she had transitioned to a healthier, happier place in life. The 60s were going to be very different from the 50s, for sure!

Self-Reflection Changes Our Very Brain

Now, through scientific research done as a result of increased technology, today's scientists are seeing that mental effort (or *mindfulness*), which generates a "willful focus of attention," can reshape the structure of how the brain functions.[1] The power of mindfulness, with its "directed mental force,"[2] reshapes our neural circuitry and critical maps. Specifically, the brain continually refines its processing capabilities to meet the challenges with which we present it, increasing the communicative power of the neurons and circuits that respond to received inputs or that are tapped for habitual outputs. In other words, mindfulness helps improve our brain's efficiency by providing the pathways between the neurons and pathways to other neurons. It is the brain's astonishing power to learn and unlearn, to adapt and change, to carry with it our experiences that allows us to throw off biological materialism. Thus, the life we lead creates the brain we have, and mindfulness becomes the transforming power of the mind to reshape the brain.

Through changes in the way we focus our attention, we have the capacity to make choices about what mental direction we will take—for instance, whether we will experience positive emotions such as love and joy, and/or reduce negative emotions such as fear and anger. When we are intentionally and objectively aware of our thoughts in the present moment, it brings our mental processes under greater voluntary and conscious control. This allows us the experience of greater self-esteem and control during a time when we may start to relinquish independence in other areas.[3]

This new understanding of the power of the mind to shape our brain can advance not only our knowledge, but also our wisdom.

Diane S. Schaupp, Ph.D.

Awakening Consciousness in Later Adulthood

As later adults, we can deepen our sense of ourselves by practicing *meditation*. Meditation is a "quieting" of the mind; a sort of mental "getting out of one's own way." It allows for a lessening of the mental "static" that is the sound of the many whirling thoughts and worries we frequently entertain.

Meditation is a central component to the experience of mindfulness. It also can stimulate those areas of the brain associated with intuition and give us improved self-control and self-esteem.

Yet, most of us grew up learning to develop an analytical mode of consciousness that severed our sense of connectivity to the environment and our communities. We now know that the *analytic* mode of consciousness is a *left brain* operation. It is equally important to develop our *right brain* capabilities, which consist of our intuition and creativity. The functioning of our right brain is enhanced by meditation, which lowers our overall brain activity and allows us to cross over into our right brain capabilities. The ability to use both sides of our brain *enhances* our human capabilities, whereas relying too much on either side of our brain compromises our functioning. We lead a more balanced life by moving back and forth between our right brain and our left brain.

If we fail to trust our intuitive insight, then we cut ourselves off from the potential wisdom we personally can bring to a situation. Often, in the accelerating pace at which we live, or in the confusion of turbulent feelings, we have too much internal static to attune to intuition's subtle signal. By becoming quieter, through meditation, we can tune in to subtle feelings and hear the quiet voice of wisdom within us.

Intuitive knowing very often comes first as a quiet feeling.

What the feeling means comes later, with continued attention and reflection.

By deepening our connection with the universality of our being, we begin to find a deeper sense of purpose and usefulness, rather than the sense of alienation and self-rejection induced by the youth culture. By attuning to our inner self and the universe, we begin to feel empowered to carry out our role as a wise member of our community rather than feel devalued and marginalized by society. By developing our intuitive capacities through wise reflection and meditation, we step beyond ourselves and begin to sense our place in the universe. The process of such wise reflection aids us in investigating larger patterns in our life that we want to change.

When people begin to meditate, they are surprised by how hard it is to keep their attention focused on what is going on in the present moment. The body may be still, but the mind is off and running somewhere else.

The goal of Buddhism (and of our lives, I hope) has to do with being fully present in the moment, aware without judgment and able to live fully in the now. Most of us will admit how difficult a goal that is to achieve. In fact, it takes our brain at least a third of a second between the present moment and our ability to be conscious of it. Being with ourselves in the moment is not an easy task.

If you notice your mind has run off, return to the present moment once again. To do this, start concentrating for a while to focus your attention so that your attention doesn't wander. Then, shift your attention to the changes you want to make in yourself. The moment you find yourself wandering off, come back by focusing on your breathing for a while to gather your concentration. Next, drop into awareness again, getting a sense in a more intuitive way of any insights that arise about what you are reflecting on.

Diane S. Schaupp, Ph.D.

Mindfulness makes clear the difference between being present and being distracted. The same realization can come to you in everyday life. Notice what is being done during the day when you are really not present. You go through the motions of being present while your mind is somewhere else. Through this observation you can become aware of how disconnected you have become from the activities of your life. Even with the moments you most treasure, the mind often speeds on to something else.

What is it that keeps us from being in the present? Sometimes the answer reveals the hidden influence of deeply ingrained emotional patterns. Often, what makes us resist experiencing emotions is our habitual reaction to them.

Neuroscientist and Nobel Prize winner Gerald Edelman proposes that emotional habits—our most familiar ways of thinking, feeling, and reacting—take shape at the neural level through the impact of simple repetitions in the connections between brain cells (thinking about the ability of our mind's attention to transform our physical brain in this way is similar to Jeff Schwartz and Sharon Begley's perspective, discussed earlier in this chapter.) The more often a particular circuit in the brain is used, the stronger the connection becomes.[4] Thus, when you have a choice between two ways of reacting, the one with the stronger web of connections usually wins out, like the well-worn branch of a fork in the road.

Our emotional patterns or habits are learned so thoroughly that they operate outside our awareness. Much of their power over our lives comes from the fact that they are largely unconscious. Just as we are unaware of the forming of these emotional patterns, so we remain unaware of how they control us. The concern here is how to change the emotional patterns that get in our way...and this is where mindfulness comes in.

The habit of attentiveness can lead us to tune out many details of our life, but mindfulness allows us to do the opposite. Mindful attention is like turning a dial to bring clarity and richness to our experience. It can notice much of what the mind ordinarily tunes out. Mindful awareness creates a kind of work space for us, a place in the mind where we can see and deal with automatic behaviors.

With mindfulness, you are no longer completely unaware of the contents of that secret compartment in the mind. You examine in a clear light what's been put into that secret compartment as it can offer clues to difficulties in your emotional life.

After a while you'll be able to see how you play out in the present learned emotional patterns from your earlier life. You'll also begin to see how you can bring empathy and awareness to these patterns. In recognizing hidden emotional patterns, you'll be able to see things clearly—not bound by conditioning, fear, or avoidance, but based on a fuller, more accurate perception.

Mindfulness helps us see what is going on in our mind without reacting to it. This awareness allows us to experience things without judgment or interpretation, without resistance. This quality of investigative awareness goes beyond the level of just thinking about what's going on to a deeper, inner listening that observes thoughts and feelings as they come and go.

By bringing thoughts and feelings under the purview of an observing awareness, we will start to see things as they actually are, rather than how we think they are. The first step in this clear thinking comes when we pause and become mindful, interrupting the flow of our habitual thoughts, feelings, and reactions.

Another way to accomplish this "quieting" is to focus on a single thought, image, feeling, phase, sound, or experience. You can do this while engaging in "conscious walking," or "walking meditation."

In bringing mindfulness to walking, you learn the sequences of unconscious habits in your activities. Mindful walking also reveals that you don't have to be sitting still to be mindful. You can practice mindfulness in the midst of life, by bringing the quality of awareness to any activity.

The point of mindful walking is not to get somewhere, but to become aware of the process of walking itself. For that reason, you need only a short path—one that allows for ten paces or so will be fine—in a room or outdoors where you can walk back and forth. To walk mindfully:

✝ Starting with your feet about a shoulder's width apart, become aware of whatever sensation you feel as you mentally scan your body, allowing your mind to become subtle in its perception. Feel whatever sensations are in your legs and feet: the pressure of your weight distributed on the soles, the sensations in each leg as you make slight adjustments to stay upright.

✝ Should your mind wander or if you become distracted, just bring it back to the sensations in your feet and legs.

✝ Now, gradually shift your weight onto one foot. Notice the sensations of the movement, the lightness or heaviness of each leg.

✝ See how accurately you can observe the actual sensations as you lift your weight to the other foot. Notice whatever you find, whether it's tightness, pressure, tenderness, or tingling.

✛ Now, slowly lift your foot and place it on the floor in front of you, shifting your weight into it, experiencing the changing sensation, the contact with the floor, the shifting of muscles as the leg moves. Continue to move forward in this fashion, becoming consciously aware of and directed towards the sensations that occur as you place one foot first, then the other.

✛ As you come to the end of your walking path, or need to change direction in walking, first be aware of standing, then of the process of turning as you change directions.

✛ Stay very self-contained through the walking, absorbed in the experience of walking and in the sensations in your legs and feet, grounded in your actual experience. When your mind wanders, return with awareness to the sensations of movement.

✛ Walk at a speed that allows you to stay mindful. If your mind is agitated or wanders a lot, try walking faster for a while. As your mind becomes more concentrated, slow down. You can experiment with walking at different speeds to find one at which you can remain aware most easily and still walk naturally.

What did you experience during the meditation? How did you feel when you first began? What do you feel like now? Has there been any change? Were you able to focus during your meditation? Aside from sensations in your feet, did you notice anything else? What do you know now that you didn't notice before? Were there any surprises? Did you have any intense emotions?

In conscious walking, you learn to step back and pay attention to your being. It helps you to step away and look at yourself and what you are doing in life with some compassion, calm, and clarity. Clarity is power. Use the time to listen to your inner voice, your regrets about things left undone, people not seen. Then let the regrets go. Lie in your grave and listen to your eulogy and ask yourself whether you would miss or want what you have shed.

But do purely pleasurable things, too, when you practice mindfulness: walk in the park, read more books, see more movies, brunch with more friends, do absolutely nothing. See to your quality of being, and you can emerge stronger than ever and ready to take advantage of every glorious moment.

Being with yourself may seem like a waste of time if you are struggling to stay afloat and you need to devote your time to paying your bills. If that is the case, spending a short time each day meditating will help you stay emotionally and mentally alert, and physically well.

"Why Do I Want to Take a Journey?"

The best way to figure out where you're going is to understand where you've been. That means revisiting the past—your understanding of it, your comfort levels with it—and then moving on.

Your stories and experiences of the past are part of who you are today. By deliberately recalling experiences of the past, you can become aware of the rhythms and patterns of your life and begin to absorb life's larger meaning and purpose. When you do so, you can start telling your story. You will find this empowering.

Time spent looking into your past and within yourself will help you affirm your life, see how the parts fit into the whole, and bring clarity to what is most life-giving and important to you. Soak up the uniqueness of your thought-provoking stories, revel in your good memories, appreciate your ability to learn and make hard decisions, and learn to appreciate life's complexities and mysteries. Your many years of living give you a fresh perspective unavailable to you when you were younger. Celebrate your journey!

Endnotes

1 Roger Walsh and Shauna L. Shapiro, "The Meeting of Meditative Disciplines and Western Psychology," *American Psychologist* (April 2006): 229-236.

2. Jeffrey M. Schwartz and Sharon Begley, *The Mind and the Brain: Neuroplasticity and the Power of Mental Force* (New York: Regan Books, 2002), p. 254.

3. Roger Walsh and Shauna L. Shapiro, pp. 229-230.

4. Gerald Edelman, *Neural Darwinism* (New York: Basic Books, 1987).

Diane S. Schaupp, Ph.D.

Chapter 3
Paths to Self-Fulfillment

In our early years, we focus outside of ourselves to accomplish important developmental tasks such as establishing our career and raising our children. Sometimes, if we are troubled with unresolved matters from the past, we seek pastoral or psychological counseling. But, more often, we lose ourselves in the hustle and bustle of life.

As we approach 60, we enter a crossroads. We can choose the path of continuing our outward focus, or we can strike forward on a path that leads inward. If we start down the latter road, we begin to identify persistent patterns that disturb our inner peace, and start to realize that we have the power to change these patterns.

When we put aside the hustle and bustle of life, we find more time and space for self-reflection. In closing the gap between who we want to be and who we really are, we can be more present and open to our lives.

Depending on what you decide at the crossroads, aging may come to mean different things. Different choices, reflections, perspectives, and acceptances as you reach the crossroads lead to vastly different outcomes. The final choice is yours; with it, aging will become:

+ a time of great possibilities and freedom,

+ a time of emptiness and sadness,

+ a time of busy-ness and outward focus, or

+ a time of self-acceptance and the now.

In Later Adulthood

Repeated soul searching helps us become aware of life's rhythms and patterns. Such inward introspection helps us discover what relationships and experiences have shaped us, and what we truly value. When we notice the many roles we have had, all the things we have done, all the losses we have survived, we can come to acknowledge that we are made up of *all* of these things.

When who we are, including our aging self, is not denied or suppressed, but instead allowed to grow in the light of who we really are, a tremendous development of our inner life is possible. Through this process, we begin to absorb life's larger meaning and purpose.

When we start to look within, we consider whether the essential nature of our personal identity has survived through time: Have we been true to ourselves, our deepest values and concerns? We evaluate the quality of our close relationships, the degree to which we have been able to meet the needs of others: Is our marriage strong and fulfilling? Does remaining in the partnership strengthen our sense of self, or would it be better to move on if we don't have a real partnership? Have we been able to give back to our mothers, brothers, sisters throughout the years? Finally, we reflect on the extent to which our philosophy of life has been translated into

Diane S. Schaupp, Ph.D.

patterns of significant action: If we care for the environment, have we tried to advance ways to preserve green acres and curtail pollution? If we believe in the young, have we promoted scholarships that give underprivileged children unexpected opportunities?

The process of accepting our past life as it has been can be a difficult challenge, yet we must be able to affirm our life just as it happened, for better or worse—without substitutes. When we exhibit such integrity, we do not compare ourselves with others who may seem more fortunate, or wonder about opportunities missed along the way. We do not ask those unanswerable questions such as "What if I did this? What if I did that?" Instead, we say quietly but firmly, "I am who I am. I have lived as I have lived."

A flexible and nonjudgmental attitude towards our life history allows us to conceive of new directions for growth and to feel optimistic about our possibility of success. Integrity and self-acceptance develop hand in hand with greater maturity.

Still, it is important not to exclude those feelings of cynicism and hopelessness and despair that are legitimate. Later life brings many quite reasonable reasons for experiencing despair: aspects of a past one fervently wishes had been different; aspects of a present that cause unremitting pain; aspects of a future that are uncertain and frightening. And, of course, there remains inescapable death, that one aspect of the future that is both wholly certain and wholly unknowable. We must acknowledge and integrate these feelings as we age. If we strike the proper balance, we can achieve human wholeness, authenticity, and soundness.

The final outcome of our self-reflection differs from person to person. Some adults who have experienced grave, lifelong trauma or suffer from serious physical handicaps manage to develop an attitude of contentment with their lot in life. Other adults come to view the past with great dissatisfaction and resentment, although their lives have been comparatively conflict free. What makes the difference depends on the degree to which we come to accept both ourselves and mortality.

Those who let despair direct their futures are much more likely to be carrying unresolved psychological baggage from the past. To experience integrity, it is necessary that we incorporate our lifelong sequence of conflicts, failures, and disappointments. This is difficult at a time when we face some degree of devaluation—and even hostility—from the social community. The negative attitudes expressed by family members, colleagues, and younger people toward the dependence and old-fashioned ways of older adults lead us to feel quite discouraged about our self-worth. Coupled with the gradual deterioration of some of our physical capabilities—particularly the loss of hearing, impaired vision, and limited motor agility—we increasingly can become frustrated, discouraged, and disconnected.

All of these factors are likely to create feelings of regret about the past and a desire to be able to do things differently. This can lead us to endless speculation about how things might have been, or about what actions might have been taken if conditions had only been different. Being ruled by despair makes the calm acceptance of death impossible, leading us to seek death as a way to end what we perceive as our miserable existence, or to fear death because it makes it impossible to compensate for past failures.

With acceptance of your life as it is, as it has been, and as it will become, you move toward inner peace. Give looking inward a try. Getting reacquainted with yourself is a magnificent gift that only you can give yourself. As you do so:

Diane S. Schaupp, Ph.D.

✝ soak up your beautiful and thought-provoking stories,

✝ revel in your good memories,

✝ appreciate your ability to learn and make hard decisions, and

✝ marvel at life's complexities and mystery.

In doing so, you can focus on the parts of you that you want and create your best possible future.

Finding Soul Silence

There seems to be a drive toward transcendence in all of us. Something in us wants to be free, and it seeks its freedom any way it can.

There is freedom in accepting who we are and what we want from life, even though those wants may not be feasible; in beginning to accept our inevitable decline and consequent losses rather than fight or deny them; in moving beyond the busy-ness of ordinary, everyday life.

Soul silencing occurs when we come to terms with matters of the past, start to identify and quiet the persistent patterns that disturb our inner peace, and journey toward positive change and transformation.

In soul silencing, we begin to get a sense of how fleeting and insubstantial everything is. We see that no experience can ever be as complete as we would like, and no object can ever satisfy us completely. In accepting life as it is with all of its paradoxes (i.e., gratifying/frustrating, sweet/bitter, pleasant/painful, success/failure, old/new), we can use it to awaken our souls. In dropping into the gap of these dualities, we can free ourselves of stress and silence our souls. Soul silencing directs our focus to the reality that our achievements in life always fall a bit short of our goals. *We come to accept the gap between our expectations and the way things actually are.*

The disparity between the way we perceive things and the way they actually are is at the root of our struggle. Once we learn to make this disparity part of our experience in our reflections, life can become our teacher. We can be more open to it rather than fighting it when it disappoints us.

How we handle the gap between our expectations and reality makes all the difference in our unfolding lives. In moments where the uncertainties and vulnerabilities of this gap come to mind, bring awareness to these times. Resist the tendency to try to control life in whatever way you usually do that. There is something more interesting and more compelling than having complete control. Our aging self has something else in store for us.

The inevitable changes with age and the losses that accompany this stage of life keep us forever striving toward personal growth, which involves uncertainty. This undercuts the need for stability, security, and certainty—something our aging self craves even as it simultaneously undermines it. Yet risking being awkward and vulnerable seems to be the only way we can move toward growth. It is how we can flourish when we age.

Balance comes when we learn to be off-balance, not when we hold ourselves aloof. From this place our inner life grows.

Diane S. Schaupp, Ph.D.

Accessing Our Wisdom

Unlike the task of youth, which is to construct a self, the later adult must break free of the personal conditions and dreams that dominate youth. The higher self, God, or society replaces the personal self as the guiding force in life. We turn from a preoccupation with status and wealth to paying more attention to our spiritual longings. As Allen Chinen points out in *In the Ever After*, while the hero (or younger self) struggles to change the world, the later adult seeks self-transformation through painful insight and authentic reformation. Where the hero seeks victory in the outer world, the later adult seeks emancipation from it based on freedom from social convention. Finally, while the hero moves "from obscurity into prominence, from the present to the future," the later adult moves in the opposite direction, "back home, into the past, and toward the deeper, more fundamental strata of human experience."[1]

The later adult uses his or her wisdom to counsel and inspire youth, helping them balance their idealistic aspirations with the practical needs of society. But what is wisdom? Everyone has a different definition. Paul Baltic and J. Smith have pointed out, "Everybody's definition of wisdom will be different in the words, but the melody, I suspect, will be the same. Wisdom consists of multiple facets. Among the more important facets are maturity, knowledge, experience, and intelligence—both cognitive and emotional."[2]

A wise person also comes to master the reciprocity that involves both caring for, and learning from, the young. Wisdom also develops as we ponder life and death.

Developing a Point of View About Death

Inexorably, we journey through different phases of life. Sometimes we are prepared for an impending death; other times death hits suddenly. We struggle against the shadow of death but it fights against our will to live. Each one of us reacts differently to death's calling. Some of us embrace it, while others of us experience anger or depression.

As we face our death, we experience our lives in a different way—as richer, deeper, more precious than we realized. We realize that we, to some extent, have caused our own and other's unhappiness, and that we have begun to take the first step toward changing things. The pilgrimage toward the essence of life has begun and becomes more vivid as we accept our mortality. As we look back, we can see a picture of our life. And we wisely understand the meaning of our life here on earth.

The evolution of a point of view about death requires some capacity to absorb the loss of one's close relatives and friends, as well as to accept one's own death. The former task may be even more difficult, in that the death of peers begins to destroy the social group of which we are a member. We see people suffer from long illnesses, die abruptly in the midst of thriving and vigorous lives, or die in absurd, meaningless accidents. In each instance, those who survive must ask themselves about the value of each life, and subsequently, the value of their own life. We are left with a growing set of possibilities about our own life. Have we lived our life to the fullest? What do we need to change if we feel we have not?

The development of a perspective about death is a continuous process that begins in childhood and is not fully resolved until later adulthood. The earliest concern about death—during the toddler years—reflects an inability to

Diane S. Schaupp, Ph.D.

conceive of an irreversible state of lifelessness. Toddlers are likely to think that a person could be dead at one moment and not dead at the next. By middle-school age, children have a rather realistic concept of death, but are unlikely to relate that concept to themselves or to others close to them.

During later adolescence thoughts about one's own death become more realistic. Before that time, we have not yet established an integrated identity. As we work to establish this, we are able to project ourselves into the distant future and conceive of our mortality. In the process, we ask ourselves about the meaning of life and the possibility of our death. It is during this stage that we begin to form an individualistic point of view about death.

In early adulthood, we form intimate personal bonds that we expect will endure. Our concerns about death at this stage include some anxiety about the possible death of the other person and emerging feelings of responsibility for him or her. Our own death has a greater consequence once we link our personal fate with that of another. At this point, a point of view about death must involve some sense of being able to provide for our partner or to feel confident that our companion can survive in our absence. Our view about death broadens from a preoccupation with our own mortality to an appreciation of our relationships and interdependence with other people.

During middle adulthood, we recognize that we have already lived about half of our life. The issue of death becomes increasingly concrete as parents and older relatives die. At the same time, we begin to have a larger personal impact on our families and communities. The degree to which we gain satisfaction from our own contributions to future generations now determines the extent of our anxiety about death. We find that experiencing feelings of personal effectiveness lessens our sense of death's threat.

Ideally, during later adulthood we come to accept our life as we have lived it and begin to see death as a natural part of the life span. As a result of having accepted our life, we come to accept its end without fear or discouragement. This does not imply a willingness to die, but an acceptance of the fact of death. As we age, we can appreciate that the usefulness of our contributions does not necessarily depend on our physical presence. Death therefore no longer poses a threat to our personal value, to our potential for accomplishment, or to our desire to influence the lives of others.

The experience of the death of others during adulthood clarifies our own life. With each death, we reflect on the quality of the relationship we had with the person, the nature of his or her accomplishments, and the essential value or contributions of our own life. The death of each loved or cherished person educates us about the meaning and value of our own life. We respond with great admiration to those who confront their own death openly and with acceptance. However, life-menacing crises such as a serious illness can produce transformations of a similar depth. I remember a woman in her 60s whom I met when I worked as a visiting nurse in New York City. As I changed her wound dressing daily, she would speak to me about the birds at her feeder or her concerns about her husband once she was gone. When I left her home, I felt more centered with God.

If we proceed on our life path with newfound humility and openness, and a real acceptance of our death, we find ourselves much more receptive to spiritual instructions and spiritual practice. We become mindful of not becoming entangled in a 9-to-5 existence, where we live without any view of the deeper meaning of life. Our task on this planet is to strike a balance, to find a middle way, to learn not to overstretch ourselves with extraneous activities and preoccupations, but to simplify our lives more and more.

The key to finding a happy balance in modern life is simplicity. The peace of mind it brings gives us more time to pursue the things of the spirit and the knowledge that only spiritual truth can bring. This, in turn, can help us face our inevitable death.

In living my life, I have come to realize that the effects of the denial of death go far beyond the individual; they affect the whole world. Believing that this life is the only one, many modern people move through life without considering how their outcome impacts all forms of living and nonliving matter.

In Early Elderhood

By the end of later adulthood, most of us have confronted our fear of death (for better or worse) and developed a point of view about death. If we have successfully examined and accepted our life through a life review, we find life at this stage begins to make sense to us. Finding personal authenticity brings a sense of personal dignity about the choices we've made and the goals we've met without a sense of despair for failures, missed opportunities, or misfortunes. Wisdom has resulted from our life and our successes and mistakes.

A new challenge is about to be faced in this stage of life, however. Even though we know that death is a certainty, there is an element of human thought that prevents us from facing the full realization of death and makes us continue to hope for immortality. At this point, a conflict builds between our acceptance of death and our intensifying hope for immortality.

Fortunately, we can come to achieve a sense of immortality through activities that connect and attach us to the future generations. Grandparenting is one way immortality can be achieved. Another way to attain immortality is through devotion to country, social organizations or groups, or humankind.

We can proceed down this path, or one that brings us to negativity, in the sense of being bound by our own life history. In place of a belief in our continuous existence and transformation, we experience resignation as an end of concern for ourselves and others.

Taking Care of the Next Generation

We can impact the next generation in a way that brings immortality in several different kinds of ways. First, we need to consider how unconscious attitudes and behaviors have contributed to today's ecological crisis that, if left unchecked, can negatively affect the life expectancy of today's youth.

In so doing, we must not limit ourselves to soul searching alone. There are things we can do to turn the crisis about. According to Thomas Berry, an environmental activist,

> A transformation of momentous proportions is now taking place that eventually will establish a new ecological balance between the human community and the earth. Because later adults have lived through the momentous changes of the twentieth century, they can serve as bridges between the old and new paradigms. With their professional expertise, economic power, and moral responsibility, they can help us make the transition from our technologically-based culture into the emerging ecological age.[3]

Diane S. Schaupp, Ph.D.

Buddhist scholar Joanna Macy, author of *World as Lover, World as Self,* urges people to awaken their ecological self, the transpersonal mode of being that shifts our identity beyond that of the human family to include the nonhuman world. We do this by broadening our sense of identity to include other animals, mountains, rivers, clouds and minerals—the whole interdependent web of life. Macy calls this the "greening of the self," an ending to our separation from nature that creates a basis for effective environmental action.[4]

This ecological sensibility inspires us to make political and consumer decisions with several generations in mind. As early elders make their inner riches available to the world, they can help spearhead the ecological movement and safeguard the survival of the planet.

Mentoring is another way that later adults and early elders can be helpful to the younger generation. *Mentoring* is the art by which later adults and elders pass on to younger people the living flame of their wisdom. Mentors do not impose doctrines and values on mentees in an attempt to clone themselves and make themselves immortal. Rather, they evoke the individuality of their apprentices, applauding them as they struggle to clarify their values and discover their authentic life paths. In the presence of a wise later adult or early elder, mentees can talk about their failures and shortcomings, indiscretions and foibles, without feeling shamed or judged.

What enables the mentor to act in such a compassionate way? As we age, the libido (life force) that propelled us toward reproduction now becomes invested in transmitting a pattern of experience larger than genes. Mentoring preserves life experiences by leaving a legacy, so that the wisdom accumulated through years of difficult learning will not disappear as our physical brain power wears out. That is why mentoring is so valuable to later adults and early elders. Later adults and early elders impart a lifetime of wisdom (including personal attitudes, moral and ethical judgments, and aesthetic appreciations) through the give-and-take of a living dialogue with a younger student.

In a mentoring relationship, the exchange that occurs is beneficial to both parties. Just as it is empowering to give, to offer another the fruits of one's learning, so it is rejuvenating to receive the stimulating energies and new ideas characteristic of younger individuals. Without such exchanges, later adults or early elders may remain locked in the past.

For the mentoring relationship to work, a mentor should not hurry to impart his knowledge to the mentee. The best mentoring involves listening to mentees. Young people frequently want to try out new ideas, and later adults or early elders can be most helpful by listening attentively and non-judgmentally, without forming premature conclusions.

Many later adults and early elders hesitate to engage in the practice of mentoring, thinking they do not have anything to offer. However, there are many areas in which expertise plays a role, and mentoring can take place in a limitless number of settings. For example, if you spent years taking care of the house and family, you can pass on the skills of how not to hurry through troublesome chores in haste, but to perform them more consciously; how to manage a household budget; and how to stay connected to all members of one's family. While mindfully modeling the "how to" of daily life, you will find numerous occasions to discuss such substantial issues as the search for meaning, career choices, marriage, and family life. Or, if you are a spiritual individual, you can offer listening and counsel to someone whose own experience with faith is troubled.

Be proud of your life accomplishments, recognizing that

Diane S. Schaupp, Ph.D.

if you esteem your experiences enough, you need to find a means to pass them on. When you become a mentor you teach more than technical information about your area of expertise. You impart lessons in the art of living that can influence your mentee's personal circumstances.

You may be wondering how to find and make contact with mentees. To make sure your special legacy is preserved, take an inventory of the skills and knowledge that represent your gifts and talents from your life experience. Once you have uncovered a match between your knowledge and your potential customers, find a way to acquaint yourself with them. For example, if you wish to pass on your spiritual experience, start participating in retreats or staying after a religious service for the coffee hour to meet more individuals seeking faithful direction in life. If it is a new perspective on chores you are passing on, engage in online chat groups about cleaning tips so that you can offer online counsel to participants, or host a community course on the easiest ways to stay on top of household chores. Ultimately, the mentor recognizes the mentee as a friend and equal.

Mentoring also has its roots inside the family, in the experience of grandparenthood. Grandparents, who are once-removed from the scene of parental conflict, often provide youth with a safe refuge. Additionally, with their understanding of the long-term cycles that govern human events, grandparents can help young people cope with the unfolding of their lives.

Consider the role of a grandmother when an adolescent granddaughter describes her breakup with a boyfriend: The grandmother, who has endured adolescent infatuation, the full spectrum of mature love, and the ripening of compassion, shares in her granddaughter's sorrow. But she also has perspective, and the knowledge that what seems tragic today may bring good fortune tomorrow. As the grandmother shares the truth of her own stumblings and eventual triumphs, she teaches that the pain and joy that her granddaughter will experience are necessary when viewed in terms of the larger pattern of our lives. In turn, as she listens to how her grandmother accepts and blesses the mysterious workings of destiny, the young woman feels reassured that if she endures, she too will one day be an inspiration to her own grandchildren.

Mentoring also enables later adults and early elders with an alternative to total retirement, letting them remain in the workplace as trainers of younger workers. "We are witnessing the end of yesterday's retirement with Grandpa asleep on the porch, the gold watch the company gave him ticking in his vest pocket, and his friends coming over later to go fishing or play cards or checkers," wrote authors Ken Dychtwald and Joe Flower in Age Wave. "Later life is rapidly becoming a time when you do not stop working completely, but instead shift gears to part-time, seasonal, or occasional work, mixed with productive and involved leisure activities."[5]

Community building is still another way to take care of younger generations. When all generations are welcomed into the circle of life, the culture becomes a healthy one. And, as historians report, later adults and early elders of society have always been the transmitters of tradition, the guardians of ancestral values, the providers of continuity. Their life histories function as a guide to the ongoing community.

Authors Jerry Gerber, Janet Wolff, Walter Klores, and Gene Braun wrote in Lifetrends, "Loneliness in aging is nothing new, but now that people are surviving into their later years healthier, less dependent, and in greater numbers than before, the possibilities of forging the spirit of community are more realistic. Current elders are laying the groundwork for a more communal old age, and of course, the baby boomers are likely to be the elder community-builders par excellence."[6]

Before considering mentoring and community building, it is important to reduce the pull of our personal ego, so we can serve others without being sabotaged by a hidden agenda of unfulfilled needs. To become a mentor and community builder, we must learn to lead without dominating others, to make compassion the ruling principle of our actions, and to serve the whole with a multigenerational perspective. Such a life-transforming process can best be accomplished in a supportive community with people who are committed to the same high aspirations.

In Later Elderhood

The attainment of interdependence arrives only after we have come to terms with our mortality by understanding that the gifts of life lose their value unless they move from one person to another. The gift of continuing to be alive, when passed onto others through friendship and mentorship, makes our spirit abundant even as our body wanes. Those who stay insular find that their spirit for life dwindles with their physical powers.

Yet, why do people cling so tenaciously to independence as they become increasingly dependent? Because all matter is in some way interconnected, it is clear that interdependence is mandatory for our survival. Why do so many of us fight it?

Accepting Interdependence

There is a tendency of some later adults to refuse to accept obvious symptoms of deterioration, mental or physical. Such refusal is apparent, for example, in a failure to take responsibility for physical needs such as nutrition and a lack of appreciation of the danger to oneself and others when the deterioration of the senses precludes such things as driving. Engaging in such denial inhibits later adults and/or elders from taking necessary responsibility for their own physical well-being and exercising their intact capabilities. It also prohibits the maturation of mutuality and interdependence in aging.

When frailty takes over, dependence is appropriate. There is really no choice but to trust in the compassion of others, and it is invigorating to be consistently surprised at how faithful some caretakers can be.

It would help those who need assistance to accept their new path if society were to redefine some traditional concepts. For example, to be "kind" ought to mean welcoming younger relatives' assistance, and to be "brave" ought to mean accepting the dependency that aging brings.

In showing youth that we can cope with increasing dependence, aging adults teach that the final stage of life can be managed. This information is not peripheral, but something everyone will need to know.

Striking a Balance

In taking care of ourselves and developing a beneficial interdependent attitude, we learn the fine art of staying in balance. Later life can be a time of gloom or a time of promise and fulfillment. There is never one particular path to follow...and the choice is always yours. Move wisely.

Endnotes

1. Allen Chinen, *In the Ever After* (Wilamette, IL: Chinen Publications, 1989).

2. P. B. Baltic and J. Smith, "Toward a Psychology of Wisdom and Its Ontagenesis," in R. J. Steinberg, ed., *Wisdom: Its Nature, Origins, and Development* (New York: Cambridge Press, 1990), pp. 87–120.

3. Thomas Berry, *The Dream of the Earth* (San Francisco: Sierra Books, 1988).

4. Joanna Macy, World As Lover, *World as Self* (Berkeley: Parallax Press, 1991).

5. Ken Dychtwald and Joe Flower, *Age Wave* (New York: Bantam Books, 1990) p. 183.

6. Jerry Gerber, Janet Wolff, Walter Klores, and Gene Braun, *Lifetrends: The Future of Baby Boomers and Other Aging Americans* (New York: Macmillan, 1989).

PART II

THE SPIRIT OF CHANGE

Chapter 4

We Have the Power

Ideally, we all want to flourish in whatever stage of life we are experiencing. To flourish means to succeed and thrive, to experience vigor, continuous self-growth, and meaning in our lives. In terms of our emotional, psychological, and social experiences, we are at all-time highs: We have strong and close relationships; we are proud of who we are and determined about where we are going; we see and feel *purpose* in our world; our health is good, both physically and mentally. And, if we work, we miss fewer days of work and are more productive in the workplace.

Yet, only 18 percent of the population is categorized as flourishing.[1] That means that while the majority function fine on a day-to-day basis, without mental or physical impairment or illness, they lack the sense of purpose, excitement, and vitality that characterizes those who flourish. Still others of us are best described as *languishing;* these individuals describe their lives as "hollow" or "empty."[2] Caught in a rut, they live life without a rudder, failing to see its purpose, and perceiving everything as tinged with gray. This is not something that any one of us would aspire to outright, but it is a state in which we may find ourselves, despite our efforts otherwise.

If your life isn't all that you would want it to be, how do you make the changes necessary to become an individual who has enhanced self-esteem, joy, vigor, and better health? Specifically, how do you become this way in later life, a time period typically characterized by unexpected and perhaps even immense changes—emotional, physical, and mental?

Fortunately, each of us has the power to respond to life's significant changes, taking us from where we are now and moving us to a better place, handling all that life is preparing to set before us. Others of us even make *proactive* changes—we look ahead and decide what we want and how to get there before the unexpected but necessary choices of later life land on our doorsteps.

Still, changing is easily said, not easily done. Change can be scary: with change comes risk, and with risk comes doubt. What is it that inspires or prompts us to make changes in our lives for the better? Why do some people just seem…*better* at it? Why are some of us flexible and personally adaptive when it comes to change, and others not?

Inspiration for Change

Crises are what alter the daily ho-hum of our lives. They upset the daily balance, placing before us differing paths that we either choose to follow, or not.

Most often, we think of the word *crisis* as a negative word, one that connotes a trauma of some sort. In this way, we can allow a crisis to get the best of us, letting it take control over our lives, our happiness, our peace of mind. Life, however, is best lived by taking what can be construed as a negative and making it a positive. This is what needs to happen with crises.

Diane S. Schaupp, Ph.D.

In altering any negative or passive mind-set about crises, and reacting to them as thoughtfully, positively, and skillfully as possible, it is important to understand the nature of the crises that we can encounter. According to Sue Monk Kidd, there are three basic sources of crises that can upset our routines and the course of our day-to-day lives. They are developmental transitions, intrusive events and internal events.[3]

Developmental Transitions

These are difficult but necessary *internal* passages that are traveled to emerge into another stage of life and become more of the individual whom we want to become. Well-known psychologist Erik Erikson believed we pass through specific life stages that present emotional issues or developmental tasks that build on the one before, and thus establish a continual blueprint for emotional growth. The amount of learning we acquire through our experiences at each stage contributes to our emotional health as we progress through life. "Development" requires a change that is lasting as we move from one stage of life to another; "transition" describes the emotional and intellectual growth experienced as we carry ourselves forward.

According to Erickson,[4] the vast majority of us successfully encounter and work our way through the following developmental transitions and emotional issues (with the last three being the ones encountered in the later years; the last stage is based on my work).

1. infancy (birth to 2 years)—basic trust vs. basic mistrust;

2. toddlerhood (2 to 3 years)—initiative vs. guilt;

3. school age (5 to 12)—industry vs. inferiority;

4. early adolescence (13 to 18)—group identity vs. alienation;

5. later adolescence (19 to 22)—individual identity vs. identity confusion;

6. early adulthood (23 to 34)—intimacy vs. isolation;

7. middle adulthood (35 to 59)—generativity vs. stagnation;

8. later adulthood (60 to 75)—authenticity vs. despair;

9. early elderhood (76 to 95)—leaving a legacy vs. extinction; and

10. later elderhood (96 on)—interdependence vs. annihilation.

An inevitable discrepancy lies between our level of development at the beginning of a stage and society's push for a new level of functioning by the end of the stage. So, if we attempt to avoid or ignore developmental transitions, we pay a high price. We need to resolve the stages successfully to emerge maturely and brimming with self-confidence.

It is important to note that developmental transitions do not go smoothly.

"Growing pains" occur at every stage of life.

For example, in later adulthood, a person experiences a tug toward youth or the need to draw on deeper, internal resources to create a revitalized participation in life. On the other side of the coin, a person faces a pull to remain static or stuck, bogged down in a life full of obligations and a lack of self-fulfillment. The person who avoids the difficult work of this transition becomes "stuck." He or she cannot resist speculating about how things might have been or about

Diane S. Schaupp, Ph.D.

what actions might have been taken if conditions "had only been different." This person may even become insensitive and hurtful.

Everyone knows someone who as that person ages becomes increasingly intolerant, brazenly insulting to family, friends, and even strangers who have the misfortune to encounter this individual. The behavior alienates everyone who knows this person. Such a person no longer responds well to the disappointments in life, and the longer this individual lives, the more bitter and angry this person becomes.

This kind of person is trapped in a tough shell of anger and bitterness. This bitterness is not a *result* of aging, although it gets worse with aging. Generally, it is a symptom of individual personality characteristics and emotional consequences that have become obstacles to his or her personal growth. The mounting bad feelings and "emotional baggage" between family and friends, and the increased alienation from them, become external obstacles to further growth. Whether it is depression, fear, anxiety, dependence, substance abuse, work pressure, or limiting relationships, until this person recognizes these obstacles and take steps to reduce their grip on his or her life, they continue to obscure this individual's resources for personal growth.

Intrusive Events

These crises come from without, and often arrive in our lives as a surprise. A death, an illness, an accident, a lost job, a broken relationship, an unwelcome move, a dashed dream, an empty nest, or a betrayal all embody intrusive events in our lives.

The positive to be experienced here is that often the

occurrence of such an event allows for an insight into our untapped potential, as we become aware of the event and work on ways to manage or to overcome it. For many of us, the confidence and sense of control that arises from our successful managing of an intrusive event bolsters our self-esteem and allows us to view ourselves in a new light. We come to realize that we have much to offer the world, ourselves, and others.

For example, several of my female friends often describe their divorces as an intrusive event in their lives. Although initially there were tears and pain, and many felt the loss of a long-held identity, a number used the divorce as a stepping-stone to accomplishing something new or different in their lives—something they never would have accomplished if they had remained married.

> Evelyn, age 49, divorced her alcoholic husband. Being a stay-at-home mom, she recognized she would have to establish herself in a career outside the home if she were to enjoy the quality of life she enjoyed while married. She enrolled in graduate school and became a law school librarian. Mary was a woman who flourished after her divorce. She now enjoys a stimulating, lucrative career, mountain scaling, and traveling around the world with new friends who also are single.

Internal Events

An internal uprising can be as simple as a vague sense of restlessness, a fleeting sense of disenchantment, a whispering but relentless inner voice saying, "There has to be more than this. Why am I doing what I am doing?" Nancy's journey (Chapter 1) began as an internal event, spurred on by a mild sense that she was not where she wanted to be and that she had spent her life in service to her family, marriage, and children. Additionally, in her case a developmental transition (she was entering her 60s) served as a catalyst. Nancy's story illustrates the obstacle to change is not aging, but emotional issues and life experiences that over time have colluded to set up barriers to trying or thinking about something new.

In fact, all of the individuals profiled thus far in this book—Nancy, Bob, Mary, and Joe—were moved to change because they were at some sort of crisis point in their lives. What was it that pulled these four people to resolve their crises positively? And in a more general sense: Why are some people able to succeed at change that would never have been predicted from their life circumstances, whereas many others in older age languish in a mild depression and isolation?

Personal Adaptability

Researchers have identified *personal adaptability* (also called "resilience" or "personal hardiness") in people as the trait that allows them to overcome adversity. Personal adaptability is the inner strength that propels some people to overcome obstacles in their path.

When we are personally adaptable, it does not mean we are free from stress, pressure, or conflict. Rather, it suggests that we cope positively with problems when they arise. We respond effectively when faced with adversity or ambiguity. We display flexibility when tasks or priorities before us change or mount. We don't hide behind others or our work, but confront issues head-on. We handle criticism, internally incorporating its wisdom and not feeling self-defensive as a result of its expression. We handle a multitude of tasks at one time without allowing feelings of stress or unfairness to overwhelm us, and we often respond to change with enthusiasm and energy. We feel a sense of purpose about the tasks in which we are engaged, and we recognize a degree of control over our world and our responsibilities.

People become *personally adaptable* by creating a set of assumptions or attitudes about themselves that influence their behaviors and the skills that they develop. They develop such beliefs that change is to be expected and that they can exert control over their activities. Yet how we cope is based on the interactions of our temperament with our life experiences. In the list that follows, I will offer the wisdom that goes hand-in-hand with fortifying our personal hardiness. These beliefs can serve as guideposts for altering the unproductive beliefs and behaviors we may possess, bringing us closer to more vigor, confidence, optimism, resilience, and receptiveness to change. They help keep us from being stuck in the same old ruts, and engender a proactive move towards personal fulfillment.

In fact, the more we come to understand the beliefs that guide our behaviors and make us more personally adaptable, the more we can engage in replacing counterproductive, self-defeating beliefs with those that lead to a more fulfilling life.

Diane S. Schaupp, Ph.D.

To Build Our Personal Adaptability...

1. *It's never too late to seek and achieve our dreams and change our lives.* Such self-knowledge guides us as we move toward our goals. It allows us to weather transitions and problems, to understand that through all of the changes in our lives, we have a core of strength to meet the challenges and take the necessary risks that enable us to grow. As the changes we make may require diligence, time, perseverance, and effort, we must root them in a sense of hope, living life in concert with our personal values.

2. **We knew what we can take control of, as Mary has done.** Stephen Covey, author of *The Seven Habits of Highly Effective People,*[5] has written that effective people focus on what they can control, spending little, if any, time and energy on matters that are beyond their sphere of influence. In other words, they focus on what they can affect every day.

In life, we do not sit back and allow others to guide us through life's passage, but move through life with a sense of purpose and personal responsibility. We do not blame others; we do not disclaim responsibility for what goes right or wrong. Maturity, a positive attitude, and wisdom are attained when we constructively determine that we are the only ones who decide the course of our lives and confidently take the reins.

At this point, I am going to offer congratulations: You have already shown some support of this belief (or at least that you are open to it) simply by reading this book.

3. *We can change our inner self-talk by reworking our negative life patterns.* We all know people who do not seem to take charge of their lives and fade instead of becoming clearer and brighter in the latter third of life. This is because they are encountering *roadblocks* to their adaptive ability. When

we repeat behaviors that lead to positive outcomes, we can call these behaviors *positive life patterns*. However, when our predictable behaviors are counterproductive or self-defeating but we continue to engage in them, *negative life patterns* are operating.

These negative patterns, which can influence all aspects of our personal and professional lives, are obstacles to our becoming personally adaptive. Often, the first enactments of negative patterns are written in childhood and acted on throughout our adult lives. Until we recognize these patterns and take responsibility for our actions, they continue to get in our way. Unfortunately, the longer they exist, the more entrenched they are likely to become, precluding our opportunities for growth.

However, when we change the internal words that prompt us and our actions throughout our life, we enhance our personal adaptability. Such changes in our thought patterns can prove life changing. Yes, consistently changing them may take time, depending on how long and how frequently we revert to the negative thought patterns. Our awareness of our thought patterns, our openness to change, and our ability to deal with obstacles that typically emerge rewards us with positive life outcomes.

When we think and feel positively, no longer viewing life and ourselves primarily through a critical lens, it enhances our intuition, creativity, and focus; affects our health beneficially; bolsters our immune system; increases our longevity; and enhances our experience of happiness while minimizing our sensitivity to pain and stress.

I want to be clear, however, that I am not suggesting that we approach life with a "Pollyanna-ish" attitude or thoughts, completely devoid of negativity. In fact, it has been shown that some negative emotions act as an anchor to reality.

Diane S. Schaupp, Ph.D.

People are able to flourish most effectively when positive emotions outweigh those that are negative on an approximately 3 to 1 ratio.

4. *We have the ability to manage stress and pressure.* Not surprisingly, a basic characteristic of adaptive people is the capacity to handle stress and pressure. This is sometimes difficult to master, as inborn temperament plays a role in why some people have a more stressful existence than others. For example, research on temperament reveals that some people are predisposed from birth to feeling stress more intensely than others.

However, temperament is not the sole variable in determining stress. Our temperament is influenced by the many life situations we encounter. In Chapter 7, you will learn more about how you can manage stress effectively by choosing when you embark on various life-changing events, at least those life-changing events that you have some control over.

5 *We accept ourselves for who we are and how we have lived our lives.* We can only find this acceptance through possessing realistic expectations and goals, recognizing our strengths as well as our vulnerabilities, and leading an authentic, balanced life in which our behaviors are in accord with our values and goals. As we look back, self-reflect, and learn to accept ourselves, we gain a clearer picture of our strengths and vulnerabilities. As we learn to articulate our values, we are in a position to remove the factors that serve as obstacles to our realizing a more satisfying life.

6. *We stay connected to others in many facets of our lives.* In the last decade, much has been written about the importance of feeling connected to others as a source of well-being and personal adaptability. Doctor and author Ned Hollowell has described in his work the power of connections and what he

terms "human moments" as a reservoir of strength.[6]

The importance of having people from whom we gather strength on an ongoing basis can never be underestimated, even if we are supremely confident and secure about ourselves. Spouses, siblings, parents, or friends all play a role. So do professional associates. In addition, when we show compassion or help others, we experience a "helper's high," an exhilarating feeling rooted in both the physical and emotional changes that result from our actions. This helps us nurture the belief that we have made a positive difference in our world—increasing our feelings of self-control. Thus, connections to other people, to values, and to causes provide the nutrients for personal adaptability.

7. *We view past mistakes as experiences for learning and growth.* Understanding and responding to past mistakes in this way does not mean we are overjoyed when we make mistakes, but rather, that we are not easily discouraged and that we look for opportunities that might be a by-product of our setbacks.

Facing mistakes and setbacks at age 60 also can prevent us from looking back sadly at lost opportunities in our lives and endlessly asking "What if...": What if I had not been so afraid of making mistakes, but instead confronted the challenges in my life? What if I had taken the other path than the one I chose? Second-guessing yourself and your past choices gets you nowhere, so don't fall into this common trap! Just as we have learned that it is never too late to seek and achieve our dreams and change our lives, so we need to learn that it is never too late to change the way we view mistakes. We can adopt the notion that most mistakes afford an opportunity for growth and learning.

8. *We take responsibility for our successes, identifying and appreciating our strengths when we succeed.* For example, we

Diane S. Schaupp, Ph.D.

observe that a promotion is because of hard work and intelligence; that our financial security after age 60 is attributable to goals and planning set up 20 years earlier; or that our good health might be partially from heredity, but also from our self-discipline about good dietary habits, exercise, and so forth. Not taking responsibility for our successes compromises any feeling of accomplishment and lessens the possibility for future successes. Further, individuals who are not personally adaptable attribute their successes to things like *luck*. How many times have you said, or heard a friend say, "Oh, I just lucked out!" Or, "I was in the right place at the right time." Or even, "Well, I have a great team backing me—that's the reason I got ahead!" Fortunately, just as we can alter our negative mind-set with regard to mistakes, so we can take steps to develop a more empowering positive attitude with regard to our achievements.

9. *We display self-discipline in our actions and how we live our lives.* When we think before we act, when we consider the feelings of others (being empathetic), when we reflect on possible solutions to a problem, when we behave in a rational and thoughtful way, when we keep from screaming at someone who has done something to make us angry, we are displaying self-discipline and self-control.

If you find you are frequently asserting "That wasn't really me," or are often apologizing for your behavior, it suggests that you experience difficulties with self-control.

Fortunately, these three steps position you to improve your self-control over time:

1. Take ownership of your behavior.

2. Think before you act. In moving from impulsivity to reflection, consider the following:

✛ What are my options?

✛ What are my goals?

✛ What obstacles might I face in achieving my goals?

✛ What new behaviors can I try to reach my objectives? (Then, when you try them out, evaluate their effectiveness and decide which to keep for future changes and behaviors.)

3. Become a proactive-problem solver.

4. Strive to act consistently over time and in different situations.

Remember, to change long-standing behavior is not easy. It takes time, and you need to prepare yourself for setbacks. Fortunately, the rewards from persevering and reaching a more balanced life are worth the struggles involved. As we become more skilled in embracing and applying the characteristics of personal adaptability, we have to continue to recognize the need to practice these skills on a regular basis so that we don't fall back into self-defeating patterns of thinking and behaving.

What's So Important to You…That You Take a Step Towards Change?

Authors and researchers Dr. Robert Brooks and Dr. Sam Goldstein say it is possible to learn to be personally adaptive or resilient at any age. We've talked about four people who were faced with a crisis in later life and were able to make changes. In each case, the changes were difficult, yet the outcomes were positive.

Nancy, for example, had felt torn throughout her life by

the need to simultaneously maintain her roles as wife, mother, and successful professional. She did not feel she had given herself enough time throughout her life to nurture herself and her friendships—or even know her husband on a deeper level. Therefore, when she entered her 60s, she was adamant that now, finally, was the time and opportunity to reinvent herself. For her, a change of location and a quieter environment would prove the keys that would allow her to achieve her goals. When Nancy embarked on her change, she finally found an opportunity to really listen to her inner voice, at which point she discovered that she had to rethink what constituted a successful life for a woman. Having accomplished what was assumed to be the role of a women in the 1950s, and the added role of a successful professional woman of the 1960s, Nancy had the self-confidence to listen to her inner voice and become a "true self" woman, one who did not measure herself by societal norms but from the depths of herself—her values, her unclaimed self, and so on.

For Nancy's husband Bob, he had felt wedged into the role of provider. He never believed he had the freedom to get to know himself better until his wife announced she wanted to take a position on a remote island. Her actions forced him into turmoil and, ultimately, into making a major career change. Then, once their last child completed graduate school, both Nancy and Bob decided they were ready to retire and create a new life for themselves. This couple had formed an entirely new perspective on life as a result of making the initial changes inspired by Nancy: They had found out they could reinvent themselves over and over again, to find a whole new world out there—or a whole new world within themselves and each other.

On the other hand, Mary's life change was precipitated by loss (also an *intrusive event*). When her husband died, she made the decision to remain in her own home indefinitely. She loved the friends she and her late husband had made together, and she knew that remaining in her own home would allow her to nurture these friendships. This was Mary's way of assuming personal control over her life—a characteristic of adaptable people. In doing so, however, she also realized that interdependence, a condition hard for some people to accept, would allow her the opportunity to realistically stay in her home. As a result, Mary has spent the last 25 years helping her friends while simultaneously allowing her daughters to support her in selected ways.

As Joe aged, he easily employed many of the qualities of personal adaptability. For example, although intellectually he remained strong, he knew that his physical limitations would erect some obstacles to his ideal path, so he maintained his desired involvement in his company by reducing the demands of his role and putting his son in charge. He also employed whatever medical or mechanical devices were available to him to reduce the impact of his physical limitations, and sought out a path that involved him staying socially connected by volunteering in schools, the community, and charitable organizations. Overall, his path included taking responsibility for his past successes and strengths and adjusting to his current physical limitations, coping well with stressful situations, and remaining connected to family and friends—all characteristics of personally adaptable people.

What about you? Are you ready to make some changes? Is there something in your life that you want to change enough that you would go through the struggles that Nancy and Bob endured? Is that change...a change in relationship that has become hurtful or dissatisfying, a change in career or environment, a change in a personal habit, or a change in educational status? If so, you understand the desire and your ability to overcome obstacles to make it happen. This book will help you to do just that in the pages that follow.

On the other hand, is your response to "Are you ready to make some changes?" more like the following: "Well, yes, but I'm too old to go back to school," or "Well, yes, but I'm used to living alone," or "Well, yes, but I've never worried about exercise before and my body still seems okay." These "Yes, but…" responses are excuses indicating that you *simply don't want to change enough to do what you have to do to make it come about.*

Alternatively, are you not sure about what you want to change in your life, but you can readily acknowledge that as of late you have been experiencing a feeling of discontent? No doubt this discontent is what led you to pick up this book. Such inner turmoil is typical of later life, and is caused by the awareness of what this time of life brings and what follows, and how much may lie ahead. In fact, many people find themselves unsure about how to face situations characteristic of later life, such as increasing physical dependency, the loss of friends and/or family members, and recognizing there is more to life than how they have been living it to this point. They also find themselves looking back on how they have lived their lives up to the present.

As a result of such questioning and the honest, often painful reflection it gives rise to, you may be encountering dissatisfaction or fear that you have not lived an authentic life. This is what gave rise to Nancy's awareness of her career dissatisfaction and how she had believed half truths about women's roles for 20-plus years. Using any newfound discomfort to examine the life path that spreads before you helps you to see how and in what ways you should change (if at all!).

When you consider making significant change(s) in your

life, it also helps to understand the various types of changes that are possible. First, there are *inevitable changes*. These are the changes over which you have little or no control, such as chronic illness, aging, or debilitating physical changes. Then there are *changes that you would like to make, but find difficult to make*. Good examples of this kind of change are deciding to lose weight or stop smoking, returning to school to learn a new skill, or downsizing one's home.

In actually initiating and enforcing change in your life, it helps if you understand that making a change is a *process*, one that can and should be worked on over time. It also helps to understand the *stages of change*, so that impatience does not take over as you carefully go about making perhaps life-altering changes.

The 12 Steps to Change

The steps described here are progressive, with each successive step building upon earlier ones. Yet people are complex. Individuals will respond to change differently. Some will be able to handle concurrent changes in their lives. This would mean that several steps are occupied, or going on, at one time. Others will struggle with one change they have identified.

As you discover these steps, you may choose to keep these words of wisdom in mind: "God grant me the serenity to accept those things I cannot change, the courage to change the things I can, and the wisdom to know the difference."

Step 1: Know the type of change. Change differs according to the scope of the change, the timing (whether it's proactive or reactive), and the degree of behavioral change and learning that must occur. To adjust your behaviors and your

Diane S. Schaupp, Ph.D.

expectations accordingly, you must acknowledge whether it is a minor or major change that you are considering; whether you are responsible for initiating the change or are simply responding to it; and come to understand how much of an impact it is going to have on the way you live your life.

Step 2: Separate the change from transition. This book is helping you think about establishing where you want to go (the proposed change), differentiating it from where you are now (the current state), and providing the information needed to narrow the gap between the proposed change and the current state.

As discussed earlier in this chapter, *transition* is the internal psychological process individuals go through to come to terms with a new change. To have a successful transition in your life, you must: (1) identify the losses associated with the change; (2) accept that you will experience both confusion and ambiguity as you determine what the change will be like and what the change will mean for you and for others; (3) support yourself in learning the new behaviors needed to achieve the change; and (4) reinforce the desired change (for example, if you are losing weight, buy a new outfit periodically to support your progress; or, take an afternoon off after spending a week at home decluttering your house).

The most difficult aspect of this stage is the uncertainty and ambiguity that transition brings. However, looking at unpredictability and uncertainty as what makes life interesting might help you on your journey toward change.

Step 3: Anticipate the losses involved in the change. Change requires ending the way things were, unlearning the old way and moving on to the new. During this part of the process, you will ask yourself, "What losses are connected to this change?" Many people feel a sense of instability and uncertainty, and stress forms as a result. Consider the example of

Nancy and Bob: There were multiple losses (i.e., the loss of old friends and colleagues, the discarding of outdated beliefs about women's roles, and the selling of their home of many years), some of which included a loss of control and familiarity (in knowing what would happen).

Changing the way we relate to others (i.e., highly emotional is one way we connect) can leave us feeling distant and disconnected at first. Tension between two people can develop when one partner grows at a different pace or direction than another; when the challenge is greater than the skill level of one or both of the partners, the relationship is at risk of being lost. Similarly, changing an addictive behavior can result in needing to change people, places, and things. For example, overeaters may need to restructure their time rather than spending it with those with whom they frequently overate. Frequently, the losses incurred at this time can feel scary.

Step 4: Deal with any emotional responses to the losses you encounter. Generally, you feel an emotional response in reaction to the perhaps multiple losses you are encountering as a result of the change. Grieving the past allows you to move on with your life. However, when your emotions are disturbing and difficult to handle, do not ignore them in the mistaken belief that confronting your emotions will lead to further distress. Such a perception impedes your progress toward your desired change.

Recognize that dealing with your emotions is a necessary step in the process towards change, and it frees you of negative thoughts and emotions, which leaves room inside to experience positive thoughts and emotions. Holding grief inside uses up the psychic energy that you can use instead for new personal growth. Additionally, it isolates you from others (whereas expressing grief to others connects you to them).

Diane S. Schaupp, Ph.D.

Step 5: Put an end to the past; move toward the future.
Sharing and experiencing feelings and emotions can be helpful, but if done to excess, can keep us "stuck in the past."
Unfortunately, there is no clear pivotal point that demarcates
the past from the present, indicating a time when focusing
on the past is no longer acceptable. For most of us, when we
remain in the past too long, it will become apparent in some
typical ways. Friends will glaze over when we continue to
bring up past events too often; partners and friends may tell
us outright that we are dwelling on the loss too long.

Your best reaction is not to immediately become defen-
sive when you hear such words or experience such criticisms.
Instead, consider them as objectively as possible, and use
them as an occasion for some work on yourself. If it becomes
apparent that you are stuck in the past and are having difficulty moving on, do what you need to do to get "unstuck."
If you discover you can't move on, or when unresolved losses from the past become apparent and have nothing to do
with current losses, acknowledge that you may require professional psychological help and support, and without shame
or guilt, go about getting that assistance.

*Step 6: Understand your personal, individual response to
change.* Once you have addressed the emotions that have
arisen as a result of the change, it is time to begin switching
from the heart to the head. The goal at this point is to understand intellectually and objectively what you have been
through and where you are in the transition process. At this
stage, it is important to understand your resistance to
change.

On the one hand, you probably know that the proposed
change is good for you. On the other, you may recognize
that you are finding it very, very hard to change. If you have
relocated, you may feel lonely. You know it was a wise move,

but making friends takes time. If you wrote a book, you may be finding it is a long process to find a publisher. If you are losing weight, you may be feeling deprived before you experience the joy of dropping to a smaller size. Acknowledge what is making it difficult for you to fully bring about the desired change.

Step 7: Experience a sense of continuity from the past to the future. Reinforcing how your needs will be met in the future through a behavioral change lessens your anxiety about that change. You see, any successful move into the future needs to be accompanied by familiarity. To leave a stage behind, you need positive feelings about the past, a sense of respect for what you can bring to a situation, and the willingness to look at what needs to happen in the future. There is no need to completely embrace the future, although thinking in this way allows your movement in that direction.

For Nancy and Bob to experience continuity, it would have been helpful for them to empathetically understand the stage of life they were leaving and the new stage of life into which they were transitioning. It also would have been useful for them to make a plan to take up some new interests together in their new location, in addition to seeking out ways to improve their communication.

Step 8: Communicate and understand the why, what, and how of your change. During this phase of the change process, you reach a point where you are willing, in your mind and in your heart, to step hesitantly into the future. The goal for this phase is to acknowledge that the old ways no longer work and new beginnings are necessary. You also need to establish during this step a sense of awareness and urgency in terms of bringing about the anticipated change. If you keep one foot in the past and one in the new, the danger is you could regress backward rather than move forward.

Diane S. Schaupp, Ph.D.

During this phase it is important that you associate with others who "walk the walk," not just "talk the talk." Their actions will inspire you to complete the change you have designated for yourself. If you have been supported up to this point, it is likely that you will begin to see the light, the *raison d'etre* for your change. You'll also be more likely to recognize the negative consequences of continuing to practice in the same old way. Associating with like-minded others minimizes confusion about your new course of action. If you don't have individuals around you to support you in your actions, seek additional mentoring or coaching to help you move toward the desired change.

Step 9: Move from confusion to creativity. At this point in the process, you feel busier than you have ever felt. Simultaneously, your anxiety begins to rise, and you might even feel slightly disoriented. Begin to create new ideas and plans to move toward the desired end point, focusing most of your energy on your change initiative. This will leave feelings of confusion behind.

The translation of your new knowledge into actual behavior is critical. Redefine the importance of cultivating an ongoing quest for learning and integrating creative problem solving, and know that you can meet and overcome any challenges.

Step 10: Create the spirit of change through a new vision. On the path to the change, new roles and/or new behaviors emerge. Clear, consistent communication that effectively describes the vision you hold of the change brings clarity to this confusing time, both to yourself and others.

Having a fixed vision provides a guiding beacon that you can fall back on in periods of ambiguity. The clearer your vision of the change, the stronger it serves as your guide.

Step 11: Create short-term wins; celebrate successes. Change occurs easiest when renewal efforts are met with positive, short-term consequences. Focusing on what you have accomplished so far, rather than what you haven't done right, will motivate you to continue making changes. In addition, small rewards, either external or internal, are helpful reinforcements to your success. When your efforts are met with positive, short-term consequences, it brings you closer to the successful end accomplishment of your vision.

Step 12: Remain consistent and congruent, and link any changes to your ultimate outcome. It is important to remain alert to the fragility of early changes and the ease with which you can regress to old ways and habits. Sustaining a change requires *long-term consistency and congruency.* To do so, keep the change you have made in the forefront of your thoughts. Early changes are fragile in terms of life expectancy, so link your new changes to any positive outcomes. The changes will begin to seep into your bloodstream. Over time, the changes become more permanent...and a new habit or lifestyle!

Now is the time to celebrate your final success!

A Cautionary Word

Change has many faces—good and bad, expected and unexpected, unsettling and time-consuming. As just mentioned, early changes are ephemeral and fragile in terms of life expectancy. Be patient and supportive of the process of change as all sorts of real and imagined obstacles get in its way—people, places, and things; fears; what-ifs; being stuck in the past; negative scripts. It simply takes a lot of reinforcement to learn new concepts and develop new ways of

Diane S. Schaupp, Ph.D.

thinking about yourself.

Here's something that will help. As you read this book, underline the phrases and concepts that trigger a response. By underlining, and reviewing what you have marked once you have finished reading, you might be able to identify areas that you want to change. For some, the changes may be small; for others, the changes will be more extensive. Remember that more time will be needed for more extensive changes.

Now, a Promise

I guarantee that the more involved you become in the challenges you face as you age, the more satisfied you will be with the experience. You will be excited as you learn the power you have inside to appreciate the remaining third of your life. Remember: The more we accept ownership for what has transpired in our life, the more empowered we become. We recognize the power of the past as well as the new growth potential within us, and find a way to continually move toward the fulfillment of our growth potential.

Endnotes

1. C. L. M. Keyes, "The Mental Health Continuum: From Languishing to Flourishing in Life," *Journal of Health and Social Behavior* 43 (2002): 207–222.

2. Barbara T. Fredrickson and Marical F. Losada, "Positive Affect and the Complex Dynamics of Human Flourishing," *American Psychologist* 60 (2005): 678–684.

3. Sue Monk Kidd, *When the Heart Waits* (San Francisco, CA: Harper and Collins, 1992), pp. 82–85.

4. Erik Erikson, *Childhood and Society* (New York: Norton, 1950), pp. 247–274.

5. Stephen R. Covey, *The Seven Habits of Highly Effective People* (New York: Simon & Schuster, 1989).

6. Edward M. Hollowell, *Connect: 12 Vital Lies That Open Your Heart, Lengthen Your Life, and Deepen Your Soul* (New York: Pantheon, 1999).

7. Robert Brooks and Sam Goldstein, *The Power of Resilience* (New York: McGraw Hill, 2003), pp. 11–20.

Chapter 5
The Past Matters

Our experience of aging can be enhanced when we value the past as well as the future. When we engage in what Pulitzer Prize-winning author Robert Butler refers to as "life review—a taking stock, a summing up, a final integration of our past—it can lead to integrity, authenticity, and integration as we come to accept our one and only life and call it our own, with all of its imperfections."[1] We can come to find meaning in it, however it has played out in the past.

If we reach 60 with major unresolved conflicts in our lives, or if an earlier phase of our development is incomplete, we usually will repeat in our present experiences our past difficulties. For example, our frantic rushing about and filling our lives with "busy" tasks is often a way of avoiding recognition of our aging self by engaging in outer, rather than inner, development. Those who fall into this trap often are inwardly fearful about what they would find out about themselves if they faced their inner unresolved conflicts from the past.

Acknowledging our earlier life history is important in determining our capacity to change and grow as we age.

Remembering our own childhood can allow us to notice when the child that we were in the past is present and needing to be remembered. By retracing our experiences, we also develop feelings for the changes we liked in our lives and what was important to us. Remembering the good times becomes invigorating, while recalling our struggles through difficult times reinforces our personal adaptability.

Yes, it is natural to want to isolate painful incidents that occur to us and pretend that they don't matter. Similarly, when strong, negative memories from our childhood are triggered—especially if we are not quite conscious of what is affecting us—we may want to push them aside, locking them up in our minds and avoiding their conscious recall. Over time, however, this can lead to our feeling increasingly out of control, overwhelmed, and guilty—all of which will serve to make us less effective in managing the day-to-day stressors in our life. We are already beginning to see how being empowered and positive helps us cope better and remain personally adaptive.

Rather than pushing painful memories away, we need to use the occurrence of such moments to reorganize what unresolved issues we have and thereby heal our memories. Although many resist making changes in themselves because they believe past experiences cannot be changed, cognitive psychologists champion a different view: present behavior stems largely from our *thinking* about the reality that originated from past experiences. Thus we can change our present behavior by examining our automatic thoughts and changing them to be more reflective of the current reality at work. This *reframing* of our thoughts, or *recasting them using more hopeful and life-enhancing words*, ultimately results in changes in how we feel and act.

Our efforts at understanding prior experiences serve to

Diane S. Schaupp, Ph.D.

diminish the difficult intensity of current and past negative moments. The more we recognize the unresolved part of ourselves that seeks expression, the less it needs to gain our attention through our self-defeating behaviors. As we become more aware of the issues that evoke our deepest responses, we gain mastery over them, and they lose their ability to move us in some way. Even the past can lose its hold over us if we choose to bring our skills of personal adaptability to bear upon it.

Life Patterns

Many patterns of thinking, feeling, and behaving have their roots in childhood experiences and impressions. For example, being bitten by a dog can leave us feeling frightened of dogs even if we have no memory of the earlier experience as adults. Or, if we had a depressed mother, it can lead us to form the impression that all people are distant and will abandon us. Usually these experiences create a repertoire of thinking, feeling, and behaving that impacts our life in self-defeating ways. The good news is we can change these life patterns.

When I coach patients in my clinical practice, it's apparent just how difficult it is to change self-defeating patterns of thinking, feeling, and behaving. Many are not aware of the negative patterns they follow. At other times, they may recognize their patterns but feel powerless to change them. When people are entrenched by unbending patterns, they are unable to direct their lives and nurture a sense of personal control. Their negative patterns interfere with the ability to create positive outcomes, especially when confronted by such crises as those discussed in the previous chapter (those of developmental transitions, intrusive events, and internal uprisings).

Coming to terms with the past by sorting through unresolved feelings and conflicts provides an opportunity to shed some of our psychological baggage and frees us to live life in a different manner. Examining the past also helps in the identification of some of our life patterns.

You also have had many pristine experiences in your life which have left you feeling hopeful. Otherwise, you wouldn't be reading this book. These are the positive patterns that become the positive foundation by which you lead your life.

Coming to Terms With the Past

There is a part of most people that lives in the past. For instance, we learn how to care for ourselves by the way we experienced our mother's caring for us. If we were adequately cared for, we learned to nurture ourselves; if we were neglected, we neglect our self-care. We learned how to relate to others by how members of our family related to one another. If necessary, we can reframe and reshape the past so that events and relationships can be "repaired," allowing us to release ourselves from the pain of the past. Otherwise, the painful past prevents us from living the full life many of us envision for ourselves.

If we work to keep past pain from our conscious awareness, it takes up a lot of psychic energy. Once we acknowledge our pain and start to heal, we seem to have almost limitless energy. So let's start "repair work" on the past now. This will move us closer to identifying the patterns by which we live our lives.

To help you evaluate what the starting point for your past self-reflection could be, take a few moments to reflect on where you are in your life's journey. Much of who we become

Diane S. Schaupp, Ph.D.

depends on how you have approached the question of "Who am I?" throughout life (this is true, even though part of your personality also arises from your genetic dispositions, and the families and cultures into which you are born). To gain the self-awareness you need to begin the repair work of the past, reflect on, and answer honestly, these basic questions to the best of your ability:

+ How does an event from my childhood affect my life as it stands today?

+ Am I interacting with others now as if I am still responding to those from my earlier relationships?

+ Do I understand myself?

+ Do I know and feel comfortable with who I am?

+ How can I go from here to where I want to go?

Alan had just retired at age 68. With more time available to be with himself, he began to realize how his wife attracted people and he did not. He spoke about how critical and perfectionistic his parents were, especially his mother. As his treatment with his therapist progressed, Alan realized, to his dismay, that he had become just as critical as his mother. He joined a therapy group, and over time started to relate to people in a more positive manner.

Many people feel like Alan—"I'll never do what my mother did"—only to realize, with a little self-reflection, that indeed they have turned into their mothers.

Heal Painful Memories or Thoughts

The process of learning about ourselves begins early in life, and although much of the questioning of our actions occurs unconsciously, asking ourselves the above questions consciously begins to make us aware of whom we are today. It creates a bridge to the past, and allows us to connect to painful experiences from our childhood.

Note: If you are having difficulty identifying how a childhood emotion relates to a fairly complex companion emotion of today, it may be helpful to speak with a professional.

An example of a life repair that you might wish to address is your relationship with your parents. (It also could be a relationship with a sibling, a neighbor, a friend, a relative—anyone with whom you experienced difficulty in your childhood.) The more difficulty you experienced with your parents in your childhood, the more crucial it is to try to find out more about their upbringing. *Realize that their failures have a story behind them that has been carried to you and re-expressed.* When you learn your parents' history, you begin to see them as fellow humans, rather than reacting blindly against them and risking replicating their hurts in your own life. No longer will their parental limitations simply provide fuel for your resentments toward them.

Diane S. Schaupp, Ph.D.

Elaine, now age 69, retired as a teacher at the age of 65. She was finding it difficult to find a direction in her life since her retirement. She was feeling socially isolated. As her story unfolded in therapy, she spoke about her early childhood, which was fraught with anxiety and fearfulness. As a young adult, she formed a close bond with her paternal Aunt Christine, who helped her learn more about her earlier childhood history. She learned that her mother had been hospitalized for depression several times during her childhood and Elaine had been cared for by other family members. Having learned about her mother's difficulties, she was able to understand why temporary separations and loss were especially difficult for her. Recognizing the source of her abandonment issues, Elaine was able to choose a career and lead a satisfactory life with co-workers and friends. It was not until she retired that her early experiences of abandonment again interfered profoundly with her life journey. She thought she had resolved these issues. Her therapist reassured her that wounds from the past never completely heal. Oftentimes, life transitions trigger the resurfacing of earlier negative life patterns. With the help of her therapist, Elaine was able to connect with the love and hate she felt toward her mother and move toward empathy for her once again. She was also able to come to terms with the realization that being in relationships meant pain from inevitable loss. She was learning that although being alone kept her from re-experiencing feelings of loss, she had to deal with feelings of extreme loneliness. As she sorted out her feelings about her losses and history of abandonment, her depression lifted and she began to reconnect with a community of friends.

As Elaine's feelings were listened to and taken seriously, and as she was allowed to express her hurt and rage, she was once again better able to make a healthy reconciliation with her mother, who was also a victim. Elaine began to see the tragedy of her mother's illness rather than simply her personal victimization.

When we remain present with the painful feelings from the past, we discover that the pain is surmountable. When we do life repair, we open up the memories, re-experience them on an emotional level, and move to a deeper level of understanding. This generally leads to movement from negative emotions to more positive ones.

You may think that keeping painful childhood memories from the past at a distance minimizes your suffering as you live your life. This is not the case. What actually happens is that *as you revisit the painful memory inside of you, it decreases in power*. Like Elaine, if you face your pain with courage, you emerge on the other side of it with a renewed commitment to life.

Much of life repair is done alone. However, it is helpful also to do life repair within the context of an intimate and trusting relationship, with someone who can accept all of your weaknesses as well as your strengths.

Uncover Negative Life Patterns

As you explore emotional patterns at work in your present life, it is important to keep in mind that many or most of your emotional reactions are probably appropriate in some situations. It is only when these reactions no longer work that they become maladaptive. *Maladaptive patterns* are often solutions used to fulfill basic human needs and wishes

—like being loved, understood, or accepted—but which prove self-defeating because they can sabotage the very attempt. The goals are compelling, but the methods are flawed. For example, we accumulate clutter to feel connected to our past, or we are critical of others to feel some sense of interpersonal control, or we express rage to avoid feeling hopeless or helpless.

Dr. Jeffrey E. Young and Dr. Janet S. Klosko describe negative emotional patterns in their book *Reinventing Your Life*.[2] The most common of these patterns are abandonment, deprivation, subjugation, mistrust, and unlovability.

At the age of 67, Ethel began to record an ethical will as a way to leave a legacy to her daughters. As she was writing it, she recognized that she had never told her daughters about the beatings she had interceded in between her father and her older brother. She decided it was time to talk to her daughters about this part of her painful history.

When she told her daughters this story, her daughters acknowledged that they felt a new closeness toward their mother. Up to that point, they felt distant from their mother because she had seemed to maintain a façade of superficial happiness that her daughters perceived as false. After hearing their mother's story, the daughters now recognized that their mother had pretended to be happy to protect herself from her painful past.

Observing Negative Patterns at Play in Your Life

You can first identify and keep track of any negative patterns affecting your life by noting those times when you suspect you are overreacting to a particular situation. At, or shortly after those moments, track parts of the pattern(s) at work in your life and ask what triggered this overreaction. For example, does your intense anger at your partner when he or she asks you to do something remind you of times in your childhood when a parent demanded that you do something? This pattern would be typical of a subjugation pattern.

In the preceding vignette on abandonment, even though Elaine had her Aunt Christine to help her heal her abandonment issues, Elaine, as an adult, still was vulnerable to deep sadness and feelings of isolation at the prospect of a temporary separation. It is likely that Elaine's mother had also experienced abandonment as a child. Oftentimes, life patterns, both positive and negative, are passed through the generations.

Opening up to and acknowledging the subjugation or abandonment pattern or any other possible negative life patterns, and bringing them into awareness through meditation and introspection, allows for a fresh breath of change. Still, such patterns may be hard to let go, even if they no longer serve any useful purpose. Don't be impatient with the process. In choosing to explore these parts of yourself, the process of inner exploration itself can open the way to living life more authentically rather than through the distorted lens of the negative emotional pattern.

For example, if the abandonment pattern seems familiar in your life, it can help you to realize that you can be both solitary *and* content, rather than feeling isolated and despairing. People with abandonment fears need to learn that they will be all right on their own, that they have the inner resources to meet their needs themselves and will not fall apart if someone leaves.

Understanding that we are no longer dependent (as we were as children) helps us recognize the "there and then" versus the "here and now" differences of our experience. Further, learning in small doses to be alone—which is more readily achieved by doing something you love to do—will make you feel you can flourish rather than languish when you are alone. Another way to empower yourself is to negotiate time spent apart and time spent together in a relationship.

As healing occurs, being especially attentive to feelings that even a symbolic abandonment stirs up will help you track this pattern as it starts to take over. Learning to trust in your connection with others reveals that you have started moving forward and beyond this negative pattern. In my clinical practice, I often remind my patients that the feelings involved in reparative work from the past often get worse before they will begin to feel better.

Handle the Pain

In reading about these patterns, it's only natural that they will stir up some pretty intense feelings. It's important to acknowledge these emotional reactions and to empathize with the part of yourself that accepts the pattern's existence in your life.

Healing, or neutralizing, these patterns in your life starts only through an unwavering look at yourself. You need to let yourself feel the underlying pain and dread, if only to realize that you can survive. Neutralizing the underlying feelings of a pattern ultimately defeats what otherwise gives the pattern its power in your mind.

Another important point: When people first hear the descriptions of the patterns, they think, "Oh, my gosh! I've got so many!" *Still, no matter how many of these patterns may come up in your life from time to time, it is advisable to work with one pattern at a time so that you are not overwhelmed.* You see, as you explore each pattern, you need a sustained resolve and honesty with yourself. Then, once you've identified the places in your life where you've kept an emotional pattern alive, you need to shake yourself out of complacency and reassess who you are and who you want to be as you challenge your own sense of self.

No doubt about it: during the process, you will feel at times like running away from it all. *Stay firm and continue your inner journey until you have a glimpse of feeling freer, of a more direct connection to your life and the people in it.* Once the pull of that greater freedom and authenticity takes hold, it becomes much harder to turn back. At some point, you will tend to go through a natural grieving as you let go of old identities, familiar habits, and ways of being. Once grieving unfolds, you emerge feeling more alive and freer than you've ever felt. You have begun to shed your psychological baggage—and psychological baggage from the past is heavy!

As the healing process continues, mindfully embrace your feelings, not evaluating them, not rejecting them, not holding on to them; just feel them naturally and let them move through you, embraced by an empathetic awareness.

Keep a journal or notebook handy so you can record your experiences and learn to recognize telltale signs of patterns as they occur. When you recognize a pattern, it is important not to invalidate your experience by minimizing it with a

Diane S. Schaupp, Ph.D.

label, such as "Oh, that is an abandonment pattern." *Categorizing in this way is a dismissal of the feelings in the moment.* Give yourself some empathy first as you recognize what is operating in your life before trying to initiate attempts to change.

Embrace Empathy

Mindful empathy means being with our feelings without trying to change them. As we experience these deep feelings, we can make connections between our memories that constitute the origins of a life pattern and our present feelings and responses. New ways of seeing our old patterns challenge our outworn assumptions and allow us to arrive at fresh insights.

Once you begin to empathize with your pattern of feelings, you will be less motivated to be overly rational or engage in emotional distancing. *Empathy makes it possible for you to see the distortions you engage in more clearly because you aren't so apt to judge yourself.* With empathy, you can begin to do some restorative work. How do you do this? Reframing, investigating, and challenging your thought patterns (discussed in Chapter 6) and gaining insight into emotional reactions is useful. Making an effort to behave in a new way also is reparative. At other times, physical expression, through which we access and free up our emotions, offers an effective vehicle. Physical expression might involve dancing, sports, or the artistic expression of negative emotions into a positive form. Relationships are another tool that aid in the healing of emotional experiences. We have already seen how a relationship with a therapist can be healing, but other relationships, such as marriage or a close friendship, can be types of healing relationships. We bring our patterns into our intimate marital relationship, so that marriage offers us a second chance to experience intimacy in a proactive way and rework our life patterns.

Once you are well on the path toward acknowledging and empathizing with your negative emotional patterns or psychological baggage, you can begin the work of change.

Work to Heal Your Relationships

Unresolved feelings about others weigh our spirits down and take up valuable space in our minds and hearts. These unresolved feelings keep us from letting go of the past and moving forward. In fact, any kind of past resentments distort current efforts toward personal growth.

A common example of an unresolved issue is the deprecating self-judgment many of us experience over how we parented our children. At some point, all parents need to recognize that they are not responsible for their adult children's behavior. Overcoming any real (or imagined) shortcomings can relieve parents of burdens that make it difficult for them to move forward. The reality is that loving parents did the best they could as parents with the tools they had.

As we start to work on this issue in our own lives, it's interesting to go back and look at our childhood and how we were parented. As we recognize our parents' history, we can identify a parenting behavior that we replicated through our parenting. Or, often, generations go from one extreme on a continuum to another to rectify a perceived unhealthy pattern. For instance, one generation of parents may be overly permissive, while the next generation of parents might be too strict. Recognizing these patterns helps later adults become effective and loving grandparents. Additionally, any

Diane S. Schaupp, Ph.D.

new role modeling we take on might help our now-adult children understand there are other ways for them to effectively parent—ways that are more mindful and moderate. This helps break the generational cycle of ineffective parenting.

When we reach back into the past to heal relationships, we find *forgiveness* to be a powerful tool. The act of forgiveness, though, often resurfaces emotional pain from the past. Many times we end up creating thoughts that justify our angry position. We feel the other party deserves to learn a lesson, and we are to become the teacher. That's because it is more comfortable to be the teacher than the victim. However, taking this position on a perceived wrongdoing does not allow us to examine our role in creating the problematic relationship or event. And forgiving another's wrongdoing requires us to forgive ourselves for our part in the situation.

Forgiveness involves far more than simply letting go of the past. It involves an acceptance of life on its terms, not ours. It also entails examining our expectations of ourselves and others that are unrealistic. As we do so, remember that part of our journey is to know our inner self. Knowing ourselves better involves an acceptance of our *shadow*—the unknown part of ourselves that trips and sabotages our efforts when we least expect it.

Unsent letters are another good tool for healing unhealthy relationships. An unsent letter helps us deal with a grievance toward someone. This strategy gives us permission to write without censorship, risk, or fear of hurting someone. According to Kathleen Adams in her book, *Journal to the Self*,[3] writing such letters provides us with the "three Cs—catharsis, completion, and clarity."

If you like, you can choose to send the letters at a later

time. Waiting a period of time often changes our emotional filter. With that change, we can evaluate whether our first thoughts were healing and restorative ones.

Turn Failures Into Triumphs

Life review also involves returning to painful memories of past failures. In doing so, we can come to understand *the unexpected growth that resulted from decisions that were the best we could make with the level of maturity we possessed at the time*. When we revisit these painful memories, we realize we garnered much strength as a result of overcoming the mistake.

It is from such experiences of growth that we become capable of mentoring younger people. We can reassure them, with confidence and compassion, that the pain won't last forever, that indeed they will make it. In continuing to reassure them, we can remind these young people that they have learned an important lesson with grace.

Many patients at 60 and after have come to my office for help in forgiving themselves and others, and for help in finding new ways of responding. For example, they learn to embrace their parents and begin to laugh about their behavior that mimics their parents' behaviors rather than take themselves so seriously and feeling resentment toward their parents. Recently a 65-year-old man came to my office to resolve some difficulties from the past, hoping that he could find some inner peace as he struggled with terminal prostate cancer. As a result of our discussion, he developed closer relationships with his children and grandchildren before he died.

Diane S. Schaupp, Ph.D.

Evelyn, age 63, initially came to my office for symptoms related to stress in her life. She noticed that she was smoking more and increasingly irritable with her family and co-workers. Evelyn had a high-pressure job. In addition, she was the primary caregiver for her 94-year-old mother with whom she has lived, along with her three children, since her divorce 30 years ago.

As we talked, Evelyn began to express feelings about her failed marriage: "At the time, I had to keep going. I could not think about my feelings." Over the next couple of sessions, she continued to express a wide range of emotions about the loss of her marriage. Initially, Evelyn felt too guilty to express the multitude of mixed feelings she had about her mother, because her mother had taken in her family at the time of her divorce. Only over time did it become clear that although she was grateful for her mother's help, she still possessed a myriad of resentments toward her mother.

As Evelyn's treatment progressed, she recognized how her divorce had forced her to take on responsibilities she never dreamed of. This awareness gave her more confidence in herself. Evelyn also became less resentful of her mother by getting out her negative feeling. She was also able to share a comfortable space with her mother. In addition, Evelyn became a more effective guide to her young adult children.

Increasingly, Evelyn became confident in her ability to make changes, as she had done 30 years earlier when she graduated from college and held a professional position while raising her three children. Once again, Evelyn found herself able to enjoy her relationships with others. She also felt sure she could manage her job, because now she recognized her strength at overcoming hardship. Evelyn came to see life from a different perspective. Realizing that business as usual would go on without her, Evelyn decided to take more time off for herself.

Turn a New Corner

In revisiting the past, gratefulness can result. There is gratitude for having done the best you could do, for having participated in the grand scheme of life, for having made a contribution to the whole. Accepting the inevitable rightness of how events unfolded, you marvel at what you learned about life and how well it turned out for you. You feel a new inner strength as you gain these insights. You may also experience a deep desire to reach out and support younger people in their life's journey. That is what happens when you make peace with your own journey.

Never forget that your attitude is everything, and with all that there is to life, don't leave your happiness to destiny. A lack of effort and ignorance, intentional or otherwise, only results in a joyless life.

The time you spend looking at your past and within yourself will help you affirm your life, see how the parts fit into the whole, and bring clarity to what is most life-giving and important to you. Soak up your thought-provoking stories, revel in your memories, appreciate your ability to learn and make hard decisions, and marvel at life's complexities and mystery. Celebrate your journey!

Diane S. Schaupp, Ph.D.

Recommended Books for Making Changes in How We Think About the Past

Anthony, Martin M., and Levinson, Richard P. *When Perfect Isn't Good Enough* (Oakland, CA: New Harbinger Publications, 1998). A workbook with strategies for coping with perfectionism.

Berm, Eric. *Games People Play.* (New York: Grove Press, 1964). Helps you identify your different inner voices, and how these various voices interact with other peoples' various inner voices.

Boer, Lee, and Rappoport, Judith. *Getting Control* (New York: Penguin Books, 1991). A "how-to" book about obsessive-compulsive behavior.

Foa, Edna B., and Wilson, Reid. *Stop Obsessing* (New York: Bantam Books, 2001). How to overcome your obsessions and compulsions.

Gray, John. *Mars and Venus Together Forever* (New York: Harper Paperback, 1996). A practical guide to creating lasting intimacy.

Helmstetter, Shad. *What to Say When You Talk to Yourself* (New York: Simon & Schuster, 1982). Explains how to change your thoughts so you can talk to yourself in a more positive way.

Jeffers, Susan. *Feel the Fear and Do It Anyway* (New York: Fawcett Books, 1987). A how-to book about facing certain fears.

Kalellis, Peter M. *Restoring Relationships* (New York: Crossroad Publishing, 2001). Five things to try before you say goodbye.

Kritsberg, Wayne. The Adult Children of Alcoholic Syndrome. (New York: Boston Books, 1988). A step-by-step guide to discovery and recovery.

Lerner, Harriet. *The Dance of Anger* (New York: Harper & Row, 1985). Describes how to change the dynamics of pursuing and distancing in intimate relationships.

Stone, Hal, and Stone, Sidea. *Embracing Your Inner Critic* (New York: Harper & Collins, 1993). Turn your self-criticism into a creative asset.

Tanner, Deborah. *You Just Don't Understand* (New York: Ballantine Books, 1990). Describes different communication styles between women and men.

Young, Jeffrey E., & Klosko, Janet S. *Reinventing Your Life* (New York: Plume, 1994). Identifies maladaptive scripts and how to change them.

Endnotes

1. Robert Butler, "The Life Review: An Interpretation of Reminiscence in the Aged," in Patrick L. McKee, ed., *Philosophical Foundations of Gerontology* (New York: Human Science Press, 1982), p. 238.

2. Jeffrey E. Young and Janet S. Klosko, *Reinventing Your Life* (New York: Plume Books, 1994).

3. Kathleen Adams, *Journal to the Self* (New York: Warner Books, 1990), pp. 172–179.

Chapter 6

Changing Attitudes, Changing Our Mind

Our attitude is our most precious possession. With a good attitude, we can learn to make the best of whatever situation we face. Our attitude can neutralize the impact of the inevitable changes and losses in our life as we age.

Often, our attitude is what people remember most about us. A person with a positive outlook on life has a gleam in his or her eye. We all have seen the person who seems to walk with a "black cloud" over his or her head, while others who walk in a positive manner seem to have good things happen to them. This is not accidental: We can cause good things to happen to us. (To find out how, just keep reading!)

Authors C. B. Pert, A. Goodheart, and E. Rossi all report on studies finding that a negative attitude undermines the immune system. Depression actually makes the body sick.[1] What to do or say to yourself to remain positive varies from person to person, but S. Kobasa and M. Puccetti discovered that people with a combination of the following three attitudes were less likely to become ill:

✝ persons who view tasks they face as challenges or opportunities;

✝ persons who feel they have choices and a great degree of control over their own fate; and

✝ persons who feel they have a purpose for living.

They reported that people with these three attitudes exhibit "hardiness." Their research also showed that this quality of hardiness was "three times more powerful as social support and exercise put together."[2]

Recently, a study headed by the University of Iowa Medical School's Neurobiology researchers identified what are called "traceable physical pathways" that are responsible for our emotional reactions. In other words, when we change a thought about an event, we create a new pathway in the brain that creates a new emotional response to that event. For instance, we have a pathway for a negative response. When we create a positive thought, a new pathway is formed, which in turn creates a new positive emotion. This process of building new pathways in the brain is similar to what happens to the brain when a limb is retrained after someone loses the function of a limb following a stroke. The exercising of the disabled limb creates new pathways in the brain. The newly formed pathways make it possible for the limb to function as it once did.

A tiny part of the brain called the amygdala plays an important role in the ability to experience emotions, as well as the ability to identify the emotions someone else is experiencing. Research on the amygdala suggests that changing our attitude even may have positive effects on our health.

It's clear that we have the power to manipulate our brains with positive thoughts. When we nurture our brain with

Diane S. Schaupp, Ph.D.

hopeful thoughts, the mind eventually comes to believe what we are telling it. This is important because our brain is not necessarily our friend: It hears whatever it is told and then it makes our body react accordingly. However, we can make friends with our brain by feeding it believable thoughts that are *positive*. Let's face it: there's an upside and a downside to everything. So, why not choose to look at the "cup as half full rather than half empty?" Feelings are an honest barometer of what we are thinking, but the thoughts we have are *controllable*. So we can choose our thoughts, attitudes, and outlook.

Sometimes, though, our own attitudes are so much a part of us that we really can't identify them or see them clearly and objectively. Or, if and when we recognize we have a problem, we don't know how to change. Let me help you unlock your inner world and attitudes and provide a life-changing pathway of growth. The process revolves around a conception called *self-talk*.

Self-Talk

Self-talk refers to our belief systems or patterns of thought. These belief systems can take the form of private speech, thoughts, or the words we speak. Some researchers suggest that we talk privately in our minds at the rate of approximately 1,300 words per minute! To make positive changes about how you think about aging, you would be smart to learn more about how you can use self-talk.

The concept of self-talk and its impact explains why someone can experience inner rest and peace in the midst of the most wrenching experiences of life. Also, it is the reason a person can ignore all the positive, pleasant events occurring in his or her life and, instead, focus on a minor worry and become miserable. Thoughts create emotions!

If our emotions are determined by our thoughts, it follows that our thoughts strongly affect our behaviors. For example, if you feel happy, you are more apt to let a grouchy word from a grocery store clerk slide off of you rather than reacting to it in similar fashion.

Thoughts determining our behavior become particularly relevant with age. For example, have you known someone who people say was "born old"? These are the people who are overburdened by life and live joylessly. Then, there are the 70- or 80-year-olds who have a glimmer in their eyes and a bounce to their step. In exploring the thoughts of both of these types of people, the findings would reveal that their self-talk contributes to their demeanor.

Consequently, it follows that if your thoughts are creating your emotions, then you can change your emotions by changing your thoughts. And that, by changing your emotions, you can change your demeanor.

You experience considerable self-control by controlling your thinking. Controlling your thoughts is done by capturing every thought that enters your mind and examining it to see if it is worthy of finding a place in your belief system. If it fails the test, you argue with it, debate it and dispute its rationality, and then get rid of it quickly.

Let me point out a common trap that many people fall into: the trap of irrational thinking. Don't accept the false idea that your emotions, feelings, and behaviors are controlled by the events in your life. You are at the helm; *you* can take control, rather than letting events control you. In the context of this book, change your thoughts and self-talk, and you change your mind for the better about your aging self.

Diane S. Schaupp, Ph.D.

Coming Face-to-Face With What You Really Think About Your Aging Self

Take some time before reading further to make a list of the kinds of self-talk you usually make about your aging self. As you look in the mirror and see an aging adult in front of you, what kinds of statements do you make about yourself? Do you say…:

✛ I hate the way my skin looks, especially my sagging chin!

✛ I can't remember anything anymore. I don't like this getting older thing.

✛ Every time I try to walk, my bones creak and I ache. It takes so long to get anywhere.

Now, write down some statements you typically make in the spaces below.

When I look in the mirror at myself, I see:

✛_____

✛_____

✛_____

✛_____

✛_____

Now make another list, writing down some statements you *want* to make about yourself. Not sure what they should be? Think specifically about reframing the thoughts listed above to more positive ones. For example:

✛ I can't remember as much as I used to but I am learning strategies to make up for my short-term memory loss.

Besides, I find I am able to think about problems in a more comprehensive way because of my life or long-term experience.

✛ It really feels great when I stretch out in the morning first and then go about my day. My body feels a lot better. I have to learn to stop pushing myself and being in such a rush; instead, I am going to take a little extra time to smell the roses and get to where I want to go without putting undue pressure on myself.

✛ I notice the texture of my skin is changing, but I can use moisturizing cream and remember that with my wrinkled skin comes wisdom that I can share with others.

The statements above are examples of positive self-talk at work. Now, write down some better ways to respond to the specific thoughts you make about your aging self:

✛_____

✛_____

✛_____

✛_____

Similarly, you can use positive, instead of negative, self-talk when you are feeling angry, depressed, guilty, worried, and anxious and/or stressed. Rather than allowing it to sink you deeper into anger, depression, guilt, worry, anxiety, or stress, have it raise you up *out* of your negative emotions and thoughts.

The following vignette illustrates how soothing self-talk can assist you in viewing past anxieties in a new light and in reframing your belief system.

Diane S. Schaupp, Ph.D.

Amanda, who is 60 years old, has always been anxious about her finances despite an awareness that she is financially comfortable. She always feels a twinge of guilt when she spends money. Although she is generous with her family, at the same time she feels fearful that she will run out of money. Recently, while visiting her mother, she learned that her maternal grandfather had lost the family home during the Depression. Her mother related, "I could remember going down to the furnace room where my father went every night. I would watch him as he nervously figured on a chalkboard how not to lose our home." Amanda recognizes that she inherited anxieties and fears about money through both her grandfather and mother. This new awareness provided her the freedom to use the tool of self talk. New self-talk now helps her manage her anxieties about money; for example: "I can afford to buy this beautiful scarf. My grandfather lost his home, but that was because of the Depression, and not because he was careless with his money or spent too much."

What Shapes Self-Talk?

In understanding the self-talk at work in your life, it helps you to understand your personal and collective history. Answer the questions in the areas listed below to further your awareness of your personal and collective history.

Personal Beliefs

+ Beliefs about myself?

+ Beliefs about others?

+ Beliefs about aging?

+ Beliefs about the aged?

+ Beliefs about the world?

+ Beliefs about God?

Collective Beliefs

+ What is my family motto?

+ Were the aged in my family active or passive?

+ Does my family care for its elders?

Be open to considering other questions and answers about yourself as they come to you. As you develop questions and think them through, you will be better able to identify some deep belief systems you picked up while growing up and that are the cornerstones of your self-talk today.

A Closer Look at Distortions

When *distortions* control our thinking, we focus too much on our positive or negative perceptions, and do not give a balanced view of reality. Specifically, our current perceptions of our aging selves are based on experiences accumulated over our lifetimes. When we have distorted messages about ourselves, we often sift through all the statements being made to us in our present reality to find those that support our beliefs. For example, you may view aging negatively because you focus on the physical declines of aging instead of the vast experience and knowledge you can bring to a situation now.

However, not all distortions are negative. Sometimes, we can distort our self-perceptions by accentuating a positive that isn't a positive at all! For example, you can focus on being in good physical shape as you age, in an effort to hide your true age and present yourself as younger than you really are. Or, like Ethel in Chapter 5, you can keep your painful past to yourself—but this might result in presenting to the world a mostly (and falsely!) cheerful self which then might keep you emotionally distant from your offspring, friends, and so forth.

When you act in this manner, an element of *denial* is at work. Denial is problematic as you age. Commonly, denial is used as a defense against the dread of aging, but denial distorts reality. It creates irrational thinking. And with irrational thinking, you cannot embrace aging as positive. Even though you are using denial in a positive direction, it is counterproductive because you are excusing a process in yourself that needs to be looked at carefully.

This is why every thought that goes through your mind needs to be examined. Nothing is exempt, not even those thoughts that seem positive on the surface. Fortunately, although it takes work at first to retrain the mind, ultimately a new belief system becomes automatic. Change is never easy, but it is almost always worth the effort.

Remember that the key to successful change is understanding your past and how it has shaped who you are today. As I've mentioned, sometimes there is resistance to looking at the past because you are afraid that you might find painful circumstances that you won't be able to handle. From my experience, and that of other practitioners, it turns out that usually this is not the case. In fact, often what is found is a beautiful butterfly within the cocoon that fear made.

Distorting memories through denial or idealizing what we would have hoped the past was—rather than what it actually was—dishonors the past, because it makes it unreal. We must become fearless in our search for the truth, knowing that the truth does indeed set us free. The truth is never an excuse to blame or to confront; it's our search and its purpose lies with us.

Understanding how your distorted thoughts affect your self-talk allows you to see the work you have ahead of you and realize that there also is hope present. When you look at your past now, if you see failures, you don't have to feel worthless. When you look at your future, you don't have to see only emptiness, hopelessness, and despair. Instead, you tell yourself with self-talk you can change your negative attitudes and opinions to more positive attitudes. Attitude is everything.

Reframing Negative Self-Talk About Aging

Reframing is the process of using more hopeful and life-enhancing words and concepts as your self-talk. The principles of reframing self-talk are clear and simple enough that you can start the process of positive change in your life right now. However, sometimes it helps to have the support of someone you can trust as you face yourself and restructure your belief system. That someone can be a professional counselor or a good friend. After all, the process of change is like running a race: When you enter the race, you forget what lies behind and you strain forward to what lies ahead, pressing toward the goal without full knowledge of how the change (winning the race) will impact you.

It is important to emphasize before you begin reframing your negative thought patterns that some events, some pain, some suffering will affect you in spite of your thoughts. Self-talk is not a magic formula. However, when you keep the power of self-talk in its proper perspective, it provides a means to change emotions and behavior, regardless of the circumstances. Still, there will be times that, despite the

Diane S. Schaupp, Ph.D.

enormity and abundance of the positive self-talk you conjure up, you won't be able to totally soothe the pain of a loss, failure, or disappointment. When suffering from such a painful loss, use this constructive reframing: "I am in great pain but I know the pain is part of grieving the loss. Over time, the pain will lessen."

In terms of aging, if you want to look forward to a satisfying experience as you age, stop emphasizing the negative and blaming everything that goes wrong on aging. Counteract any catastrophic statements you hear or find yourself muttering with less extreme statements.

Practice reframing your negative self-talk to positive self-talk through these examples (which are often imbued with a bit of good-natured humor):

Negative Self-Talk	Positive Self-Talk
"I can't stand to look at myself in the mirror. I always find another wrinkle."	"Another wrinkle; a sure sign of my wisdom!"
"I didn't sleep well. Drat, so many aches and pains."	"I'll take it easy. I'll take a walk. That always makes me feel good."
"I'm over-the-hill. It is downhill from here."	"I'm over-the-hill and I'm picking up speed."
"I'm so stupid. I can't understand these medical insurance forms."	"These forms are really complicated. I'll get some help with them."

"My son hasn't called. I'm such a burden."	"I haven't heard from my son. He must be so busy. I sure do miss him."
"I look like an old bag."	"I'll never win a beauty contest, but this old body certainly has served me well!"
"I am scared to death about retirement."	"I'm so excited to think of all the options I'm going to have when I retire. It's like starting a new life."

The difference expressed in the above examples about aging's physical impact is the difference between "ego transcendence" and "ego preoccupation,"[3] or between making some sort of reasonable peace with our body, and treating physical aging as our enemy or our master.

"Could people's attitudes toward aging influence how long they lived?"[4] was a research question that psychologist Becca Levy asked participants of her study in the late 1980s. Dr. Levy collected death records to find out the age at which a study participant died, or if a participant was still alive. When she matched up the records with the survey answers, she found that people with more positive views of their aging lived an average of 7.6 years longer than people with more negative views.

According to Levy, the negative stereotypes of aging and the elderly that permeate our culture could have serious consequences that go beyond just making people feel bad. For instance, in a more recent study, Becca R. Levy, Martin D. Slade, and Thomas M. Gill investigated hearing loss among aging Americans. They found that participants with negative thoughts about aging tended to lose more hearing over the course of three years than seniors with more positive views of aging.[5]

Levy says she does not know the exact mechanism by which positive attitudes translate into sharper hearing and a longer life. It may be that having a positive yet realistic attitude about aging will probably lead a person to consult with a doctor at the first sign of trouble, avoiding serious problems.

A New Attitude Toward Aging…An Autumn Harvest

You are entering a time of life in which new beginnings are possible, more than ever. Not only are you transforming your life by understanding your past and why you think the way you do about your past, but you have learned to change your reactivity about your past through changing your self-talk. Now you are challenging your thinking about your aging self as you move toward 60 and after.

As you begin to reframe your thinking to more realistic, positive thoughts about your aging self, here are some reflections and uses of metaphors that you might find helpful in developing your new belief system—it's as if you are finally able to enjoy the harvest in autumn.

Awareness

With our new awareness of the tremendous opportunities we have as we age and live our life, we have a heightened sense of presence toward everyone and everything around us. It is an attentiveness and a realization that *each moment has both purpose and potential*.

This awareness does not have the same color as life's

spring. Autumn seems to have a contemplative character to it, and everything is slowing down, undergoing a transformation from the frenetically active and productive to a more settling-in quality. This quality has been nurtured by experience, and by living and learning from decades of joys and losses.

To be aware, it is necessary to understand both the beauty and frailty of life.

Dealing with issues of the past has freed us to move beyond our egos and find our place in human history and the universe. In the process, we break free of society's conventions and begin to follow the dictates of our own hearts. This awareness enhances our understanding of the sacredness of each moment of life...which is the grace of this season. It is time to bask in the colors of autumn.

Wisdom

Awareness leads to insight, to a wisdom that transforms random circumstances into meaningful experiences. Wisdom depends on a full cooperation of knowing: observing, logical analysis, kinetic and sensory experiences, behavioral learning, and intuition. But wisdom is not a given in later life; it is a result that is nurtured and tended to throughout life. If we start experiencing it, we begin to truly celebrate autumn's harvest.

Purposefulness

In the later years of life, *productivity* gradually evolves into *purposefulness*. No longer is our work life acceptable as a daily pathway for us. It becomes important to be more selective in what we do with our time and with whom, and where we commit ourselves and our resources.

Being productive in the secular sense of earning money, owning more, and getting ahead becomes less important with age. Instead, we begin to focus our energy on what matters to us. What matters tends to be relationships, the needs of others, and the legacy that is left behind.

In the autumn harvest, there is an awareness that another season is coming to an end. For many, there are fewer years left than were lived. This is a wake-up call, transforming us from life as usual to purposefulness. There is a realization that there are things to do here while there is still time, before the uncertainty of winter is upon us.

When we find ourselves with someone who has a terminal illness, the finiteness of time really hits home. Yet the true reality is, all of us are terminally ill; it's called mortality. Realizing this, what do you choose to do in the autumn of life? Treasure loved ones? Make amends? Rediscover your spiritual self?

Gratitude

Gratitude humbles us to the generosity of the universe. Earlier in life, there is a tendency to think that the universe revolves around us. As life moves on, and we experience changes and losses that we know are completely beyond our control, it begins to dawn on us that perhaps we are not the center of the universe after all.

The realization is simultaneously troubling and comforting. Troubling because we like being in control; comforting because, even though we won't admit it, we are getting tired of ordering the universe. Hopefully, it is gratitude that we experience when we recognize the limited control we have in the universe—a simple "thank you" can serve as simple acknowledgement here.

Now, we are free to experience and be present for the simple moments in life—when looking into a child's eyes, when gazing at a flower, when listening to music, when laughing, when crying. At every moment, we are grateful for that moment.

Complex Riches

Later life is a period of complex riches: a time of great transition and opportunity; a time to remove the filters and masks we may have put in place when we were younger; a time to heal wounds; a time to reap the benefits that we've worked so hard for; a time to enjoy hard-earned pleasures. *If we've been dreading old age, it is time to reframe that belief.*

Getting older has a lot of positives. We can finally discard frenzied living and linger with beauty in ways that our hurried life did not allow previously. Later life can be a time of great authenticity, with less need to please others or to put things off. Discarding the pressure of pleasing others often becomes possible for the first time in later life. We are our own boss. In later life, we are closer to tapping into our unconscious mind. After a lifetime of rich experience, we are better able to appreciate our similarity or connectedness to others.

Remember as you read on, *our attitude is our best asset.* With all the mysterious unknowns and losses in life, the one thing we can have control over is our attitude. We can decide to make the best out of any situation we face.

Attitude is a dynamic, perceptual process. It is never static.

Making an effort to remain positive in attitude gives us an upper hand. Bad things happen, and we need to work through the pain of the grieving process, letting the sad or mad feelings surface before we can get on with living life freely. However, if we don't develop the capacity to look at the bright side and refuse to dwell on misfortune, we simply make life more difficult for ourselves. The right attitude can neutralize the negative impact of difficult circumstances.

As a reminder: reframing is the process of using more life-enhancing and hopeful words and concepts. It is important for us to reframe what getting older means to us. How we choose to age depends on *our* values and beliefs, and ours alone. Then we will find multiple pathways for our journey.

If you are ready to take on a new skill, move to the next chapter and learn more about taking control of your life.

Endnotes

1. Candice B. Pert, "The Wisdom of the Receptors: Neuropeptides, the Emotions, and the Mind Body," *Advances: Institute for Advancement of Health*, 3 (3, Summer 1986): 8–16.

Annette Goodheart, "Laugh Your Way to Health," *Science of the Mind* (September 1988): 15.

Ernest Rossi, *The Psychology of Mind-Body Healing* (New York: W. W. Norton, 1986).

2. S. Kobasa and M. Puccetti, "Personality and Social Resources in Stress Resistance," *Journal of Personality and Social Psychology* 45 (4, 1983).

3. Robert Peck, "Psychological Development in the Second Half of Life," in Bernice Neugarten, ed., *Middle Age and Aging* (Chicago, IL: The University of Chicago Press, 1968), pp. 91–92.

4. Becca R. Levy, "Mind Matters: Cognitive and Physical Effects of Aging Stereotypes," *The Journals of Gerontology Sciences and Social Success* 58 (2003): 203–211.

5. Becca R. Levy, Martin D. Slade, and Thomas M. Gill, "Hearing Decline Predicted by Obvious Stereotypes," *The Journals of Gerontology Series B; Physiological Series and Social Success* 61 (2006): 82–87.

Chapter 7

Knowing Where and When to Take Control of Your Life

How you live and exert control in your life is up to you, and only you. A great many gerontologists have come to the conclusion that *helplessness*—defined here as being unable to control or affect one's own life—is the key to physical and psychological deterioration and decline. When we are in charge of our lives, we experience less of these kinds of decline.

It's quite obvious that not everything is under our control. We can't prevent physical illness or the loss of a spouse; the means to support ourselves financially does not appear magically when we wish it so. As aging occurs, however, we gain the wisdom to understand what we can and cannot control. We also can learn how to approach and respond to situations with a different attitude and perspective in a way that benefits us the most.

Earlier in this book we learned "attitude is everything." If we didn't have a positive attitude about aging, we could change our self-talk so that we could improve our attitude. Similarly, when we encounter in later life an unexpected crisis, a difficult situation, an unfortunate passing—and the stress that goes hand in hand with such situations—we can learn how to manage the stress in a more self-enhancing way. We can choose when, and if, to make changes in response to the crises, and even how to change our attitudes about our ability to make those changes. After all, the best way to flourish is to take responsibility for our lives, to make our own choices, to be our own positive self-manager.

> "We who lived in concentration camps can remember the men who walked through the huts comforting others, giving away their piece of bread. They may have been few in number, but they offer sufficient proof that everything can be taken away from a man but one thing—the last of the human freedoms—to choose one's attitude in any given set of circumstances, to choose one's own way."
>
> —Holocaust survivor and psychiatrist Dr. Viktor Frankel

For some of us, taking charge may not be a new way of acting. Throughout our lives, baby boomers have focused on making personal choices that work for them rather than simply accepting traditional ways and customs. There is no reason that the value we have always placed on personal control and choice should not continue into the later years. The communication revolution, the changing labor market, the dramatic changes that continue to occur in the family, the globalization of most aspects of life, and the accumulation of personal wealth that gives us more of a say in how we live our latter years cannot fail to impact our perception of personal control.

Diane S. Schaupp, Ph.D.

What we want to impact, however, what we can impact, changes throughout our lives. Early in life, we usually seek out *primary control*, striving to make an *external* change in our immediate environment about something important to us, such as improving our golf skills. But as we age, and age-related biological and social challenges provide obstacles to the things we most desire to control, *secondary control* starts to increase in importance. With *secondary control*, we aim to improve and increase in strength that which is *internal*: our motivational and emotional resources. Continuing with golf as an example, if our strivings to improve our game fail, we tell ourselves that such skills are only minor indicators of our overall capability and we start focusing more on being knowledgeable about the rules of golf.

If we apply personal control to the early stages of a disease such as cancer, we exert primary control through remaining optimistic and aggressively fighting the disease. If we reach the later and irreversible stages of the disease, however, we can exert secondary control to focus on finding purpose in our life as it currently is, enjoying each moment, and perhaps putting together advanced directives for an end we can no longer avoid or deny. We may continue to strive for primary control in such areas as pain control, but in terms of secondary control, we have developed self-protective strategies to guard our emotional and motivational resources, and to support our disengagement from a goal that now may not be attainable (putting the cancer into remission).

As to handling stress on a daily basis, there are a number of different ways we can manage the stressors effectively. Let's take a closer look at stress now, how much of it there is in our life, and our response to it.

Putting Stress in Perspective

Stress is a daily part of our lives. It is prevalent among us all, regardless of age. In fact, life without stress does not exist today. *Stress* can be defined as any event or circumstance in life that requires a person to adapt or change.

Our physical body responds to stress automatically. No doubt you've heard of the instinctual "fight-or-flight" response to danger. That "danger," as we refer to it today, is stress.

Central to the fight-or-flight response are two tiny adrenal glands. When a stressful situation is encountered, the pituitary glands release a signal that tells the adrenal glands to release one or two types of hormones into the body. One hormone is released in the presence of sudden stress; another hormone, with prolonged stress. These hormones help regulate the amount and distribution of body fluids, maintain blood pressure, conserve energy, cope with infection, and allow other hormones to work more effectively throughout the body. The adrenal glands are assisted by other glands and the body's nervous system.

When we think of stress, most often we think of a situation that is affecting us negatively. Yet not all stress is bad. Stressors can be positive or negative. This was documented in an extensive study by Drs. T. H. Holmes and R. H. Rahne of the University of Washington Medical School. For example, the stress of planning a wedding can be a positive stress, whereas the stress of losing a job is usually a negative stress. Or, buying a second home or taking a vacation are positive stresses while being told we need cataract surgery or have high cholesterol are negative stresses.

Those running the study then catalogued a list of life-changing events that seemed related to physical illness and

Diane S. Schaupp, Ph.D.

mental illness. They identified 43 events, and put them together to form a scale called the "Social Readjustment Rating Scale."[1] This scale has the ability to predict the onset of disease and disability in some people. Each of these 43 events were given a numerical value.

If you score below 150 points, you are on the safe side. The stress you've been experiencing in your life is not likely to impact you physically. If you score between 150 and 300 points, your chances of becoming ill or disabled during the next two years are about 50–50. That's a moderate percentage, so you'll want to learn how to manage stress more effectively. If you score over 300 points, your chance of becoming ill increases to 90%, so again, you'll want to learn more about managing stress effectively. (For more information, go online to wikipedia.com.)

I think we all understand that overstress can make us sick. Carrying too heavy a stress load is like running our body past its maximum capacity. Like something mechanical, sooner or later our body will break down. What breaks down depends on where the weak links are in our physical body. (These links are largely inherited characteristics.)

So, how can knowing where you are on the scale benefit you rather than scare you? Although there are some changes that you do not have any control over, there are other changes you could decide to postpone. For example, if you already have numerous stressors in your life, you may choose to put off buying a second home until your life settles down a little, or delay your pursuit of remarrying. Similarly, it's good not to make significant changes to your life for a while after losing a spouse. That assumption makes sense given the results of Dr. Holmes and Rahne's research. For instance, if you lose your spouse (100), automatically there is probably a change in your financial status (39) and social activities (19).

If you decide to take a vacation (13) and make an appointment with a counselor to cope with your grief (45), this will still involve further changes and increased stress. The stress points in your life are now at 216. Other inevitable changes are lurking, too, like losses of friends or illness. It therefore makes sense to carefully control the many changes that you might be tempted to make, such as relocating or making a business change, until some of the stress in your life fades away with the passage of time.

Here are some other ways to manage the stress in your life so that it does not overwhelm you.

Using Self-Talk to Reframe Stress

Another key to surviving stress—besides postponing changes in your life—is self-talk. For instance, if you have angry or guilty feelings about the changes impacting your life, then your stress levels mount. If you reframe these negative thoughts to more realistic, positive thoughts, then self-talk becomes a coping strategy that is under your control. It helps you survive the stressors in your life.

Here are several steps you can take to begin to gain control over stress using self-talk:

1. Identify, and make a list of, the stressful situations in your life. Situations that trigger feelings of anger, depression, worry, or anxiety are all stress-creating situations. Or, identify your stressors by looking at what you are *avoiding*. What situations do you wish would disappear from your life?

2. Take one of these events, or one theme, and begin to work on your self-talk as it relates to stress. Begin by figuring out how this stressful person or situation is

Diane S. Schaupp, Ph.D.

threatening or frightening you. What are you saying to yourself already in your self-talk that triggers these feelings of threat and stress? For instance, you might be dreading making a change in your living situation. If so, begin to identify your negative self-talk. List all of the negative statements on the left side of a piece of paper. Be as specific as you possibly can. They might look something like this:

Negative self-talk:

1. I hate to make a change. This home has so many memories.

2. I never make good decisions.

3. I feel this change will put me one step closer to the grave.

4. I am shy, which will make if difficult to make new friends.

Look for any demands in your self-talk, as well as the absolutes, like "never" and "always." Then, put the paper away for a while and go on to step number 3.

3. Use your imagination to visualize yourself in the situation you've identified without an experience of stress or threat. Mental pictures are a part of self-talk, and create a great potential for change. Stress and negative self-talk are often crystallized by mental images created in the imagination. Changing those mental images reduces their power to keep us from making a change. Seeing yourself coping or changing can help you make that behavior a reality.

To do this, begin by selecting one of the stressful situations you want to change. Then, set aside between 15 and 30 minutes when no one will disturb you. The next step is to find a place to lie down, close your eyes, and be comfortable. Take some time to relax, either by using deep breathing or progressive relaxation to the muscles in your body. *Progressive relaxation* involves first tensing a group of muscles, then letting them relax. Some people do this by starting with their toes, relaxing these muscles, and then moving up their body slowly, making sure every muscle is as relaxed as possible. As your body becomes very relaxed, however, be sure your mind stays alert while directing the relaxation process.

You also can help your body relax by picturing a beautiful, tranquil scene in your mind. When you have the scene painted in your imagination, move yourself into the picture. Sit by a tree, or if you're on a beach, sit alone on a long stretch of white sand near some palm trees bending in the breeze. Watch the gentle waves come to the shore as you sit there. Try to hear the wind and feel the sun's warmth. Then concentrate on the details of the scene, noticing the flowers or the patterns in the sand. Be as present as you can be—as if you're really there.

There is another way to change your perception of a given situation. For example, if a stressful situation involves a member of your family, perhaps one of your children, try to see the situation from his or her point of view. What do they see happening? Try to visualize what they are feeling. See them as scared and vulnerable. As you do this, you may notice your own perceptions of the situation changing. Changing your perceptions about a situation is essential in the process of controlling stress.

Sometimes a situation cannot be altered or changed by

Diane S. Schaupp, Ph.D.

you, but still you are not helpless in this situation. In such a case, instead of visualizing yourself making positive changes in the situation, see yourself as successfully coping with the stress. To do so, keep your eyes closed, and take yourself to a relaxing place. Stay there in your imagination until you feel relaxed, and then go back to the stressful scene. Stay as long as you can until the stress returns before going back to the relaxing place, and then take some time to relax and feel calm and confident before opening your eyes. If you continue to practice this technique, the stress will gradually begin to ease.

Here, too, as you visualize yourself successfully coping with the stress, you might begin to understand the feelings and attitudes of the other people involved, allowing you to change your perception of the stressor. Or, you might try to identify self-talk statements you can make to yourself that would help you cope with the stress.

When we relax, different parts of the brain turn off; the parasympathetic portion of our autonomic nervous system slows our brain. This process short circuits our stress response. The relaxation response lowers our blood pressure and pulse.

4. Go back to your sheet of paper, and rewrite the negative self-talk statements by making them positives. You should be able to do this because in your imagination you have seen yourself successfully cope with the stressful situation you are facing.

Consider creating a diary of stressful situations to identify and record your stress-producing self-talk. Then, spend time using your imagination through guided imagery, and watch yourself successfully cope with or change these situations. As you discipline yourself in this way, you will be able to reduce the negative effects of stress in your life and use stress as a positive force, enabling you to take more control over your life.

Negative Self-Talk	Positive Self-Talk
1. I hate to make a change. This home has so many memories from my life.	1. I usually don't like change, but this time, I'm looking forward to it.
2. I never make good decisions.	2. I am preparing myself with information to make a good decision.
3. I feel this change will put me one step closer to the grave.	3. The change will improve my quality of life and help me enjoy each moment of my life.
4. I am shy, which will make it difficult to make new friends.	4. I am slower to make friends than some people, but I make deep connections when I do so.

The Value of Control

Research suggests that personal control in areas of life that can be influenced leads to physical and emotional well-being. A study conducted between 1992 and 1999 indicated that people who believe they make a difference in the role they value most, whether as a parent, spouse, friend, or community volunteer, actually live longer than those who don't experience the same sense of control. This research was conducted at the University of Michigan on 884 retired women and men ages 65 and older.[2]

For most people, living a meaningful life is at least as desirable as living a longer one. Being in the role most important to you may actually help accomplish *both* goals! However, since age-related declines in health and social function can reduce the number of roles you're able to fill and alter the ways in which they are carried out, it's healthy to focus one's efforts on the role or two that you enjoy most and perform best.

Such roles can be found almost anywhere—in the family or in the community, for example—and they can change as your circumstances change. Having a strong sense that you can successfully manage the role *you* value is what is important. It even may be as central to a long and healthy life as having strong bones or a healthy heart.

Now let's look at those areas of our life where we may most like or need to exert our personal, individual control.

Taking Control of Our Environment

Innate in all of us is a desire to control the environment in which we live. Evolution plays a part here, because possessing such a drive is adaptive and critical to our survival. When we influence events in our environment, we are able, for example, to find a mate, care for our offspring, and come by both shelter and food.

When we consider environmental control in the context of aging, research from the past 20 years conducted in nursing homes, in retirement communities, and among individuals suffering various traumatic events has shown that *autonomy*, or the extent to which we are able to make our own decisions and choices about our activities and when and how we engage in them, affects not only our performance and well-being, but also the physiology of our aging.

Ellen Langer of Harvard and Judith Rodin of Yale[3] did an experiment on the impact of personal control at one of the best nursing homes in Connecticut. In this study, the patients, ages 65–90, were randomly assigned to two different floors. On one floor, the patients were told, "You should be deciding how you want your rooms to be arranged… whether you want to rearrange the furniture. You should be deciding how you want to spend your time…whether you want to visit your friends in your room or their rooms. We're showing a movie two nights next week, Thursday and Friday…decide which night you'd like to go, if you choose to see it at all." The residents on the other floor were told, "We've tried to make your rooms as nice as they can be…we want to do all we can to help you. We're showing some movies next week. We'll let you know which night you're scheduled to go." Each resident was handed a plant to keep, but "the nurses will water and take care of it for you."

Three weeks later, the first group showed a significant improvement in alertness, activity, and general well-being (as rated by themselves and their nurses), while the comparison group showed a negative change. These results reveal that senility and diminished alertness are not an inevitable result of aging. In fact, the results suggest that some of the negative consequences of aging may be delayed, reversed, or possibly prevented by returning the right to make decisions. The effect of losing control over our life can be infantilizing and gives us a sense of learned helplessness. When we are given some control over change, such as choice of timing or which living arrangement we want, we experience greater psychological health.

Diane S. Schaupp, Ph.D.

In another study, Robert Schulz, Carsten Wrosch, and Julia Heckhausen reported that late elders living independently in a community showed high levels of mastery in certain areas. It seems that people in later life redirect their attention from less critical areas of their lives—volunteerism or a part-time job, for example—to those areas necessary to their own survival and interdependence—areas like meal preparation, bathing oneself, and doing light housework like the dishes, making their beds, and dusting. This study suggests that as people age and their resources dwindle, they gradually relinquish primary control in some areas of life so available resources can be devoted to maintaining control in other domains.

Social Support

A dog is man's best friend—but so is our friendly neighbor, our spouse, a relative, a long-term friend. In later life, the help and assistance given by those in our social network in response to a stressful experience does not erode our feelings of personal control; surprisingly, their efforts on our behalf actually help reduce our feelings of stress and restore those same feelings of control. This seems like a paradox, but it's not.

When others around us help define the problem, develop a plan of action, and assist in implementing the plan for resolving a stressful experience, it reminds us that this problem situation—and others—can be controlled and overcome. Research has proven the truth of this.[5]

Having a well-functioning and intact support system is key to dealing successfully with many types of personal challenges, whether it's paying the bills; deciding whether, where, and when to move; or figuring out what we need if we are planning on going on a trip. *Social support* can be defined as support that is accessible to people through social ties to others. It facilitates coping when an individual is experiencing stress, and the more social support a person receives, the greater he or she is protected, or buffered, from stressors.

Yet not everyone is a willing recipient of social support. Some older adults may resent or be offended when they are offered help. They interpret the assistance offered as a statement that they cannot cope. In this sense, social support, even though well intentioned, may create more problems than it solves. A key to aging well and gracefully is learning to accept—not resent—help that is offered.

Unfortunately, much conspires against friendship in later life. Retirement removes the context from which work friendships drew momentum. Physical problems may interfere with the nature of our activities as well as the frequency of our contact with others. Above all, the deaths of friends may rob us of the will for friendship. After too many losses, when our friends beckon, we are reluctant to put in the heart and the energy, only to have death once again deny our friendship. Yet it is our commitments to others that binds us to life. Those who stay insular find that their spirit for life dwindles along with their physical powers. The gift of continuing to be active, when passed on to others through friendship, makes the spirit abundant even as the body wanes.

The height of our engagement in later life with those relationships we regard as the most meaningful serves as a measure of emotional well-being. When core social network ties remain stable yet the more peripheral ties are pruned, this reflects older adults' exercise of control over their social lives in a manner that preserves emotional health.

Another way to take control over our life is to reframe the

Diane S. Schaupp, Ph.D.

inevitable changes of aging from a negative view to a more positive spin. We feel helpless when viewing the inevitable changes of aging negatively. Likewise, we feel empowered when we view them positively.

Adjust Personal Control

When our potential to attain particular goals is reduced, a general sense of efficacy may be preserved by downgrading the importance of these goals. Conversely, feelings of hopelessness and depression will be more pronounced when the individual maintains his or her commitment to the chosen goal.

Thus, accommodation or adaptive skills in what is important to us should serve to maintain a general sense of control. Later adults who foresee their skill level diminishing may want to consider reducing their goals to accommodate their remaining physical and time limitations, and to abandon other equally attractive options. For instance, leaving one's long-term home and moving to a more manageable apartment or closer to a caregiver can ultimately provide a sense of mastery in one's environment. By making proactive decisions about what we can manage, we can live with a renewed inner peace. At the same time, we feel empowered because we made a decision on our own rather than forced into a decision by someone else.

Endnotes

1. T. H. Holmes and R. H. Rahe, "Social Adjustment Rating Scale," *The Journal of Psychosomatic Research* 11 (1967): 213–218.

2. "The Importance of Doing What's Important to You," *Women's Health Watch* III (6, 2001), February, p. 1.

3. Ellen Langer and Judith Rodin, "The Effects of Choice and Enhanced Personal Responsibility For the Aged: A Field Experiment in an Institutional Setting," *Journal of Personality and Social Psychology* 35 (12, 1977): 897–912.

4. Robert Schulz, Carsten Wrosch, and Julia Heckhausen, "The Life Span Theory of Control: Issues and Evidence," in S. H. Zarit, L. I. I. Pearlin, and K. W. Schaie, eds., *Personal Control in Social and Life Course Contexts* (New York: Springer, 2003).

5. G. Caplin, "Mastery of Stress: Psychosocial Aspects," *American Journal of Psychiatry* 138: 413–420.

Diane S. Schaupp, Ph.D.

PART III

COURAGE

Chapter 8

Embracing Autumn Change

Time does not wait for anyone. Each day, as the clock ticks, we change. As we move toward age 60 and after, we face numerous age-related changes. Just as the gorgeous bounty of autumn color reflects a change in the season, so do changes in our sexuality, intellectual vigor, roles in marriage, work, and leisure, physical strength, psychological health, and creativity reflect age progression. Yet, we cannot only cope with such "autumn" changes, we can embrace them and turn them into positives. After all, positive thoughts lead to improved self-esteem and self-worth, while negative thoughts lead to feelings of hopelessness and depression.

In the pages that follow, I'll cover the six age-related changes mentioned above, and show how we can reframe any negative perceptions we have about their arrival and influence into positive thoughts.

Sexuality

Negative thought: "I am no longer able to enjoy sex because my vagina is dry and my husband's penis is not as erect as it used to be."

Positive reframe: "Our bodies have changed, but we can still enjoy sex."

In many cases, later adult women have healthy sexual appetites. However, the low estrogen and testosterone levels that occur with menopause can decrease sexual drive as well as the blood supply, affecting lubrication of the tissues in the vulva and vagina. Painful intercourse can result, which leads some women to avoid initiating or engaging in sex. Then, the body changes caused by age itself can decrease sexual desire. The new anxiety many feel in terms of body image can inhibit both sexual performance and sexual pleasure. Moreover, some later adult women are influenced by negative stereotypes about sexual activity in later life.[1] The postmenopausal women from my childhood wore shapeless dresses, had bluish hair, and wore black tie oxfords, announcing to the world that they felt emotionally and sexually flat.

Many older men retain the ability to achieve erections, have orgasms, and release semen at orgasm. However, aging gradually affects sexual function so that erections occur less often, do not last as long, and are less rigid. The penis itself becomes less sensitive to touch. After orgasm, the penis becomes limp more rapidly and having another erection takes longer. In addition, the volume of fluid ejaculated usually decreases, and/or ejaculation can occur with little forewarning. Male sexual drive may drop off, too, because of the decrease in testosterone levels that comes with aging. Older men sometimes feel pressure to perform sexually before they

Diane S. Schaupp, Ph.D.

or their bodies are ready, and the resulting distress may make it more difficult for them to perform. Performance anxiety can further reduce a man's ability to enjoy sexual activity.[2]

How to best handle these changes? First, remember that medical treatment is available for both women and men, depending on the cause. Although many shy away from it, it is always a good idea to discuss issues regarding sexual functions with a professional, i.e., primary care physician, gynecologist, urologist, and mental health professional. Modern medicine does make available medications that increase and prolong penile engorgement, as well as lubricants and creams that can be applied to the vaginal area to aid in sexual enjoyment.

As the pressures of middle adulthood fade—specifically the demands of career and family—couples often reinvent their earlier relationship, which can lead to increased emotional and sexual intimacy. In addition, the normal decline in sexual drive, especially for men, can provide an opportunity for a greater valuation of more diffuse forms of sexuality, greater tolerance for one's partner, a capacity to be more attentive and responsive to a partner's needs, and the possibility of a more diffuse but psychologically fulfilling response. For example, engagement in traditional sexual intercourse no longer need be the rule or standard; more creative expressions of desire, including oral sex, mutual masturbation, and the exploration of skin eroticism, can be acceptable, and sometimes even more satisfying, alternative avenues for both participants, particularly when the effective communication of individual needs and desires occurs.[3] The experience and enjoyment of one's sensuality can continue on into the latest of ages.

Intellectual Vigor

Negative thought: "I can't remember anything! I will turn into an old person who can't be trusted to do anything more than rock the day away in a rocking chair."

Positive reframe: "There are some changes in my short-term memory, but I will use some tricks to compensate for them so I can continue to be mentally active and reliable."

Memory, reasoning, information, problem-solving abilities, and mental rigidity or fluidity all influence our ability to reminisce, to assess our personal histories, and to plan for the future. Moreover, declining competencies with age have been identified in a number of areas, including reaction time, verbal learning ability, and short-term memory.[4] It becomes harder for us to remember that doctor's appointment, locate what we need at the store, or find the car keys. Memory functions are especially likely to be disrupted under conditions in which information is presented rapidly and contextual cues are absent.[5] For example, recently I had to renew my nursing license online, and I became frustrated with the speed and newness of the experience.

Yet an observational aging study conducted under the auspices of the National Institute of Mental Health revealed that those who survived 11 years (in the absence of disease) after a prior study possessed a "flexibility of mindset and actions, greater ideational freedom, imaginativeness and the organization of ideas."[6] Additionally, there was a "remarkably high quality of mental functioning."[7] Although declines were evident, what stood out was the survivor group's residual capabilities, or their abilities to acquire and adapt new knowledge, concepts, and skills. Thus older individuals may be getting less credit than they deserve for the extent of their intellectual, perceptual, and personality strengths and capabilities.

Diane S. Schaupp, Ph.D.

Well-known psychologist B. F. Skinner has described environmental qualities that may impact later adults who do not exhibit systematic thinking and fail to embrace or generate new ideas. A primary one is that many of these individuals live alone. They lack the diversity of social interactions that produce the ability to think abstractly while remaining grounded in present reality.[8]

Another area that needs to be considered when it comes to intellectual vigor is the time spent talking about the past. On the one hand, reminiscing helps sort out one's life and move towards growth. On the other hand, a preoccupation with nostalgic reminiscences does not encourage thinking in new directions. Skinner claims that one is more likely to repeat oneself as one gets older, and he therefore suggests that it may be important for later adults to move into new areas of work or play to prevent the repetition of old ideas.

Skinner also firmly believes it is possible to analyze how the quality of one's thinking is being influenced by the circumstances of aging, and to identify those interventions that can prevent the deterioration of cognitive abilities. For Skinner, such interventions include: attempts to be sensitive to signs of fatigue; planning for regular opportunities for stimulating verbal interactions with others; making careful outlines of written work to avoid distraction; and acting on ideas as they come to one's mind (rather than counting on remembering them later).

All in all, there is evidence for some decline in various aspects of cognitive functioning with age, but the deterioration is not always of very great magnitude. As we may fall into habitual patterns of thinking and acting, however, we should plan for regular opportunities for stimulating intellectual activities such as auditing a college course, working a crossword puzzle, engaging in a new activity such as baking, and verbally interacting with others to circumvent this tendency.[9]

As for tricks to compensate for one's declining intellectual vigor:

When new skills need to be learned, practice that is distributed over time encourages more efficient learning than when the same amount of practice is fit into a short space of time.[10]

People without memory problems use external memory aids and other methods to help them process and organize the vast amount of information available in the technological age in which we live.

As we age, aids can help us highlight information that might otherwise be missed: a small recorder (Dictaphone), a Filofax (organizer) or Palm Pilot, and a cell phone that can be used as a reminder for appointments, times to take medication, etc. Appointments are recorded on a Dictaphone, entered into a Filofax or a Palm Pilot programmed into the cell phone when needed. Ongoing information also is recorded on a Dictaphone or a cell phone. Each evening the information from the Dictaphone or cell phone can be transcribed into a journal. In addition, the use of a series of sticky-backed, Post-It notes and a menu chart to ensure we do not eat the same foods several days in a row can be helpful.

Internal strategies such as mnemonics also are examples of compensations used at one time or another by the majority of the population. For example, we remember how many days are in each month by repeating the rhyme that begins, "Thirty days has September...."

Learning via a mnemonic device is almost always quicker than learning through repetition.[11]

Diane S. Schaupp, Ph.D.

Further, today there are microcomputers linked to a conventional computer memory and by telephone to a paging company, although these are expensive.

Another good example of an external memory support is a name tag. Remembering name–face pairings is viewed as one of the most difficult memory tasks faced by young and old alike, and thus a likely candidate for training with mneumonics.[12] A reasonable idea would be to provide this type of environmental support universally, by adopting the practice of wearing name tags.

"Brain Gym" (http://www.braingym.org/about.html) was created for learning-disabled children and adults, but has a wealth of information for anyone who wants to enhance his or her brain functioning. There are Web sites such as http://www.mybraintrainer.com that are geared toward making your brain sharper.

Role Transitions

In later adulthood, there are likely to be role transitions that change our responsibilities, actions, and ideas about who we are on any given day. For example, there is "role loss," which comes about through widowhood, retirement, and the loss of friends through death or relocation. At the same time, new roles can emerge, requiring that we form new patterns of behaviors and relationships. Such roles can include the role of grandparent, community volunteer leader, and retiree. Let's explore some areas in later life in which roles are likely to alter.

Work and Retirement

Negative thought: "I am going to retire. I will be bored and not have enough money."

Positive reframe: "Retirement offers me an opportunity to develop new interests. If I find I run short on money, I can find work that has flexible hours."

For most of us, the work we do defines who we are. When we are asked to tell something about ourselves, frequently we describe the work we do. So when we think of retirement, there is a sense of loss on many levels. Not only do we lose a sense of a ready-made identity, but we also lose a ready-made community of friendships and tasks that express our strengths and talents. Therefore, "pre-retirement is an important time for us to evaluate what our work means to us. When making your pre-retirement work assessment, consideration of the following areas is helpful: meaning of money; meaning of duties; purpose and routine; social aspects; and identity, prestige and power."[13]

Many later adults view, or come to discover, that the traditional nonworking retirement can be emotionally unsatisfying, and they do not want to stop working. Increasingly, they are choosing what they consider a better blend of work and leisure at this pivotal point in time. Fortunately, the corporate overemphasis on the perceived strength and eagerness of younger workers is being balanced now by a new appreciation for the social judgment, personal skills, accumulated experience, low absenteeism, and ready availability of later adult workers.

Yet redefining the traditional notion of retirement lies both in restructuring the way in which we interweave work and nonwork, as well as the way in which we work (for instance, starting to work shorter days and/or taking more

Diane S. Schaupp, Ph.D.

frequent and longer time-outs).

Work patterns also are changing based on increasing life expectancy and better health among the aging population. With the ending of mandatory retirement, later adult workers have much more flexibility in choosing when, and whether, to retire.

The ideal career path across a life span may well be a career path where one cycles in and out of several different careers throughout life, each interspersed with periods of rest, recreation, retraining, and personal reflection. "A cyclic career path would provide time to spend with family members at significant points in the life cycle such as time to be present during one's children's formative years and/or time to be with ill or elder parents."[14] This can provide a foundation for how to live and find fulfillment in our later years. Comments Ken Dychtwald and Joe Flower, authors of *Age Wave*, "Although no one has yet conducted a study of the number of people who are shedding the confines of the linear life plan for the more diverse and flexible choices of the cyclic life plan, I am convinced that this is the wave of the future."[15]

According to psychologist Melissa Dittman,[16] one of the retirees she interviewed commented, "There is no right way to retire. Many people think retirement is wonderful, and for people who want to retire, that's the right thing to do. If you don't want to, that's the right thing too....I still continue to work [at age sixty-two] because I enjoy my work. Working at a later age runs in the man's family: His father worked full-time until age seventy-two, and part-time until age eighty-five."[17] Additionally, many later adults are choosing to work because they need to supplement their income as a result of inevitable changes in Social Security.

Dr. Nancy Schlossberg notes that retirement can take

many forms. She has identified six primary forms based on her interviews with about 100 retirees—although the paths retirees choose can vary over time. She reports, "the longer you live, the more paths will shift and change."[18] The forms are: Adventurers, Continuers, Easy Gliders, Involved Spectators, and Retreaters.

Retirement also encompasses a new psychological state—a sense of withdrawal from the job or the work organization and a new emotional orientation toward life. For some, retirement can prove a tumultuous time similar to adolescence because it redefines Who am I? For this reason, many women's organizations have formed around the challenges of retirement. These groups offer practical advice, a forum to challenge assumptions about retirement, and intimate conversations reminiscent of the consciousness-raising groups of the 1960s.

Retirement also can bring about stress because it is a powerful transition in ones life. To minimize the stress of the transition, work on taking your time; taking on only one change at a time; and evaluating what you are willing to give up and how you will satisfy what you don't want to lose.

In closing this section on psychological issues of work and retirement, it is important to identify the inner thoughts that lead to the turmoil typical of this stage. You see, often our work becomes a defense against the real or anticipated losses of our youth and relationships that make life meaningful. On the other hand, work in some form can be a period of giving back to society the lessons, resources, and experience accumulated and articulated over a lifetime. Retirement itself can be a vehicle for adjusting to and developing the serenity that you need to experience the imminence and inevitability of the death of peers, as well as your own passing.

Diane S. Schaupp, Ph.D.

To successfully resolve the work dilemma in later life, in my opinion, encompasses a flexible work schedule interspersed with periods of rest, recreation, and personal reflection.

Leisure Activities

Negative thought: "I am not someone who wants to spend the rest of my life playing golf."

Positive reframe: "I am grateful to have time to make new friends at my art class, but I am also grateful to have time to get to know myself better now."

Today, more than 85 percent of America's women and men over age 65 do not work. More Americans have been living longer, healthier, and more leisure-filled lives, as evidenced by an explosion in membership at country clubs and senior centers. Eighty percent of luxury travel in America now is purchased by people over age 55.

Also, more and more adult Americans are discarding a traditional, work-centered way of life and pursuing a more balanced lifestyle. The key to this shift is an increased emphasis on leisure not just as a means of rest and play, but also as an opportunity for lifelong training, continued personal growth, and the expansion of oneself through service to others. This move toward a more equal blend of work and leisure is an optimal arrangement because it provides us with an opportunity to remain actively involved in a productive, stimulating life while providing us with the rest and fun to nurture our body and soul.

Relationships

Negative thought: "I feel lost since my husband died and my grandchildren live so far away."

Positive reframe: "I have always enjoyed people. I will continue to make new friends, many of whom also will be single. I will volunteer at the nearby school to help children learn to read."

Intimate Relationships

Intimate relationships make a profound difference in the quality of life at any age. Yet in later life, the making and keeping of friends can be more difficult. In retirement, later adults often become cut off from a constant community of friendships in the workplace. Long-standing friends move away, and retirement from work can create a host of interpersonal tensions as couples find themselves having to relate to each other "24–7." Finally, there is no experience as devastating as the death of a spouse or a close friend.

Longer life spans and attitudes that are more accepting of divorce are accelerating the trend away from lifetime marriage to that of having several mates (serial monogamy) over a lifetime. Yet the shortage of older men gives rise to an unusual mix of later adult social arrangements, with several women dating the same man perhaps, or women dating younger men. Additionally, our longer life expectancies are transforming the child-centered family into an adult-centered family, with great-grandparents, grandparents, parents, and young adult children in addition to aunts, uncles, and young adult nieces and nephews.

In the following sections, I explore how the autumn of

life offers a wealth of opportunity in many relationship areas.

Marriage

Later adulthood offers couples an opportunity to rework marital relationships. For most of us, it is a time when family and career no longer dominate our time and psychic energy; we can concentrate on ourselves and our partners. Couples begin to rekindle a bond of friendship as a result of their shared history and newly acquired leisure time and interests, and they begin to renegotiate the division of daily chores with each other.

According to psychiatrist and author David Guttman, "The gender distinctions get blurred as the last children are launched in the parent's middle years. Thus, when maturing children are demonstrating that they can assume major responsibility for supplying their own physical and emotional needs, the stringent requirements of parenthood are relaxed; fathers and mothers can then reclaim the strivings and capabilities that conflicted with the parental assignment and therefore had been either repressed or lived out vicariously through the spouse."[19] In other words, during child rearing, each partner is constricted in developing his or her own personality. One partner generally assumes responsibility for the nurturing role while the other assumes responsibility for providing material resources. Once the parenting function has been completed, each partner can continue to develop all aspects of his or her personality.

In addition to changes in gender-role definitions, stresses are brought into aging marriages from numerous other arenas. Not only does the heightened awareness of death's closer proximity create new levels of anxiety, but couples also become tense about changes in their sexual performance, appearance, capacity to remember and create, and in their relationships with others. These inevitable age-related changes contribute to the individuals in a couple blaming each other for their problems.

There are various options for working out these marital issues. We can talk to friends and our partner and recognize other couples have similar struggles; we may seek psychotherapy either as a couple or as individuals; or we may choose the option of divorce.

Divorce

Divorce may bring role loss and social isolation as well as financial loss. Even when divorce is perceived as a desirable solution, the period from the suggestion of divorce to its conclusion involves a variety of painful decisions and conflicts.

Often people who experience divorce go through a period of self-analysis. During this period, they try to integrate the failures of the marriage with their personal definitions of masculinity or femininity, their competence as a loving person, and their long-held aspirations to enact the role of wife or husband. Developing these strategies to cope with the losses of divorce may prove helpful:

+ increasing one's social network;

+ understanding what went wrong in the relationship;

+ learning more about one's self by auditing classes or seeking personal counseling;

+ expressing feelings;

+ becoming more self-sufficient—for example, taking over tasks originally delegated to one's spouse; and

Diane S. Schaupp, Ph.D.

✝ more involvement with family and home activities.

It is noteworthy that while divorce requires time for grief, it also offers an opportunity for personal growth.

Widow/Widowed

Marriage provides a structure to life. It determines the way one interacts in the world, providing social roles and shaping one's identity. Death destroys all of that. The chief supporter in one's life may be gone now. For all these reasons, the death of a partner can be the most devastating event of a lifetime (outside of the loss of a child).

The early days following such a loss are filled with feelings of shock, numbness, and denial. Mourners report that it feels like they are removed from the scene, as if watching a play through a gauze curtain. Finally, the curtain rises and the pain seems worse. It feels as if life will never be normal again. The miracle of human nature is that life eventually becomes normal again.

Still, loneliness ensues, with the most ordinary of activities, such as eating and sleeping, becoming exercises in absence and isolation. Research conducted by author Robert DiGiulio[20] revealed that women who had a close friend adapted to death and to the changes easier than did those who lacked support. Reciprocity plays a part here. As time passes, the support drifts away unless the bereaved starts to offer back nurturance and attention.

Any death creates a web of complicated feelings. Anger is present among them, whether it's anger over something that happened while the person was dying, events that occurred during the course of the relationship, or simply that the living feels abandoned by the dead. Guilt is also present (for the usual reasons), but relief too can be present. Relief exists for many reasons, most often because of the difficulty of the caretaker role or because the marital relationship was difficult.

Many people avoid painful memories and feelings by idealizing the deceased. In most cases, such idealization is strong at first but it tapers off. Eventually, remembering both the good and bad is possible. Once these two aspects are remembered, integration occurs, and feelings of love toward the deceased partner return.

Progressing to get beyond the loss of a loved one takes time, and leaving your past behind may feel like a betrayal of your loved one. Over time, you can come to recognize that the past and the love you felt will always be with you. Letting go means having the fortitude to move forward toward an unknown future.

Moving forward also means incorporating some aspects of the deceased into yourself—such as continuing to appreciate the symphony, which was your partner's love—as well as learning to appreciate some traits of your spouse that you formerly did not. You also may have to let go of some aspects of your identity that were linked to your loved one, as creating a new future means coming to a fuller sense of your own individuality. It happens when widows and widowers do something as small as rearranging the furniture. It happens when they make new friends. It happens when they start dating. It happens when they go someplace new.

Diane S. Schaupp, Ph.D.

After 60 and Single

Beginning to date can be a strange experience. It's more than being out of practice—times have changed! It's a challenge to meet new people, and there are different ways of doing this than in the past (think online). No matter how old you are, you'll feel like a teenager when having to contemplate dating again.

For today's later adult women and men interested in new romance and companionship, there is a variety of ways to approach the problem of finding satisfying love relationships. What can you do to meet people? Take a job, or volunteer at a place where people gather and where you'll have a good time even if you don't meet anyone. Later adults meet through Internet dating, personal ads in the newspaper, and/or video dating services. In the 21st century, these are absolutely acceptable ways.

And don't be too hasty to discount romantic possibilities: You can be a younger woman with an older man; an older woman with a younger man; or an older woman with an older man. You can live together without getting married, or not. You can have several same-sex friendships and/or romantic liaisons, or even be one of several women dating one man (in light of the marked imbalance in the number of older single women to single men, you can expect significant changes in social and personal behavior).

Grandparents

Grandparents have the job of loving children for who they are in the moment. For the most part, grandparents are not about power and fame, but rather about love—perhaps the purest and the least exploitable love that humans can feel for one another. Grandparents teach the importance of living in the moment....Grandparents often find the smallest aspects of their grandchildren's behavior important.[21]

Grandparents are our historians. They are keepers of our collective memories and the repository of stories, the connective tissue between generations. This sense of family to which one belongs is crucial to one's identity.[22]

It is noteworthy that children of today often have several grandparents spanning the generations. With the reconfiguration of families through divorce, additional grandparents are a product of these reconfigurations. Therefore, today children have more grandparents than in the past.

It is easy to see how valuable grandparents are to grandchildren, but grandchildren are just as important to grandparents. Grandchildren give us the opportunity to pass on our values and wisdom. They also give us back the unconditional love that many of us need as we age. Grandchildren also symbolize an extension of our personal influence that will persist well beyond our death. To this extent, grandchildren help us feel more comfortable about our own death.

If for any reason you do not have grandchildren, there are foster grandchildren programs in many areas. In addition, there are numerous volunteer programs that provide opportunities to interact with children. Lastly, if you are uncomfortable with children, animals are a way of obtaining unconditional love. Recent research has emphasized the importance of pets to our health and well-being.

The new roles that we encounter in later life require a redirection of our energies, and this involves both flexibility and personal adaptability. It is quite impressive how readily people adapt to new roles for which there is little preparation or social reward.

Diane S. Schaupp, Ph.D.

Physical Strength

Negative thought: "I find it difficult to continue my activity as before, because I get tired so easily."

Positive reframe: "I am grateful that I have the wisdom to set priorities of what is important in my life so I don't wear myself out in any one activity."

Because of a change in muscle tone as we age, our overall body begins to sag, affecting our physical appearance. The physical diminishments of aging may seem insignificant or petty when compared to other issues we face as we grow older, but they are not. And if our health begins to deteriorate markedly, some of the physical problems we encounter may become painful, debilitating, and shaming.

These disconcerting changes force us to refocus from other, perhaps more interesting, aspects of our life to the demanding requirements of our body. Our responses here can vary greatly. We can experience frustration and depression, for example, or we can belligerently deny any changes to the point of neglecting our bodies and our health.

A belligerent denial of one's aging can cause undue painful consequences, especially as it relates to accidents. For example, an elder with impaired vision or reaction time may eventually become involved in a car accident that injures himself and/or others if he continues to drive. On the other hand, a resignation to one's physical diminishments that goes hand in hand with the new choice of a sedentary lifestyle can cause a premature withdrawal from life, accelerating the aging process.

I find a middle-of-the-road approach is best when it comes to physical changes. What this requires is accepting who and what we are with proactive compliance. What I mean by "proactive compliance" is that we can use our familiarity with human development to anticipate the inevitable changes that will occur as we age, approaching them with acceptance and an appropriate plan for coping with them.

Let's cover the most common of these changes now. With advancing age, hormonal changes are apparent. Women grow facial hair; men's beards grow slower. Women may become flat chested, their voices deepen, and their facial features sharpen. The estrogen that may have once inhibited dominance in one's relationships decreases. The breasts of elder men grow, their faces soften, and the testosterone that may have once facilitated dominance decreases. How these hormonal changes impact one's gender-role redefinition is not exactly clear, but we do know these hormonal changes impact our sexuality. It also is conceivable that gender role changes are attributable, in part, to these hormonal changes.

In George Valliant's study of human development of over 25 years, he assessed factors prior to age 50 that predicted healthy aging.[23] The protective factors were: not smoking, healthy weight, the absence of alcohol, some exercise, good coping skills, a good marriage, and adequate education.

Valliant's findings suggest that we have some control over the components of healthy aging. The study also suggests the importance of working to maintain our physical capabilities as best as possible through exercise until our bodies are too fragile to exercise. Then, once we can no longer drive and/or exercise, we need society to provide safe walkways in the street and public buildings, and ramps and resting places in public buildings. It is important to consider the elders in our communities, so they can continue to participate in the give-and-take of community life. After all, later adults and elders with consistent involvement in community life after age 60 continue to interact socially, and thus age successfully.

Diane S. Schaupp, Ph.D.

Recently, the National Institute on Aging has been addressing the question of why some people age well and others do not, often heading along a path that ends up in a medical condition known as frailty. Scientists are surprised to find that, in many cases, a single factor—undetected cardiovascular disease—is the major reason people become frail. Cardiovascular disease may have partly blocked blood vessels in the brain, the legs, the kidneys, or the heart. Those obstructions, in turn, can result in exhaustion or mental confusion, weakness or a slow walking pace.

Investigators say that there is a ray of hope in these findings: if cardiovascular disease is central to many of the symptoms of old age, it should be possible to slow, or delay, or even prevent many of these changes by treating the medical condition.

Researchers believe that if these findings are right, then the condition may be prevented or delayed by not smoking, by keeping cholesterol and blood pressure levels low, and by staying active. It is also important to maintain regular medical checkups. REMEMBER TO POINT OUT THESE CHANGES TO YOUR PHYSICIAN.

Psychological Health

Negative thought: "I am losing control of my life through all the changes I am forced to make because I am aging."

Positive reframe: "With the loss of my youth, I am gaining a greater appreciation for who I am and how I fit into the universal scheme of life."

Psychological health is a component of aging you can change. You cannot change earlier trauma encountered in your life, but you can take the time to rework areas of your life that impede your personal growth. To facilitate the maturational process, you have to ask yourself whether you are satisfied with who you are; if you are able to accept your own mortality and eventual death; and if you can recognize the inevitability of age-related changes. A positive resolution of these questions will enable you to acquire the wisdom to give back to society and prepare you for your ultimate interdependence on others.

Remember that *you can change your attitude about life.* Some of us do not have a positive view of age and aging, while others do. Positive aging means to love, to work, to learn something you did not know yesterday, and to enjoy the precious moments remaining with yourself and with loved ones.

This section focuses on aspects of psychological health, so it is important to mention the problems of alcoholism, depression, and anxiety in the aging population. Later adults are less likely than younger people to drink heavily or to be alcoholics, but as the aging body processes alcohol differently and has a greater effect on the aging brain, more aging adults are hospitalized from alcohol-related problems than for heart attacks. Drinking even in small amounts can cause sleepiness, confusion, poor coordination, and unsteadiness. If we take control of our alcohol intake, despite our genes, we will have a healthier chance of aging well. If you are having difficulty limiting your alcohol or drug intake, contact your state council on alcoholism for a list of referrals to clinicians specially trained in treating substance abuse problems.

As to mental health disorders such as anxiety and depression, these can develop for the first time in later adulthood as a response to losses and/or worries. Depression differs

Diane S. Schaupp, Ph.D.

from ordinary sadness in several ways. For some, depression involves a nagging sense of feeling sad that drags on as one performs daily activities. For others, it is a heavy shroud of despair or emotional emptiness that becomes debilitating.

Anxiety is internal nervousness or worrying, which can develop for no apparent reason. Anxiety can interfere greatly with one's quality of life and ability to perform daily activities. Everyone experiences nervousness or worry occasionally, but if you are suffering from chronic anxiety or depression, contact your state psychological and/or psychiatric association for a list of referrals of clinicians who are specially trained in treating depression and anxiety disorders.

Seeking professional help can alleviate some of the psychological symptoms you have struggled with for years. Professional psychological help can also reinforce positive adaptive coping skills. Positive adaptive coping skills result when we are able to strike a balance between our emotional experience and reason. Later adulthood is a time when the past can truly become the past, and emotions of serenity, joy, pleasure, and excitement can fully come into being. Narcissism may transform into humor, wisdom, and the capacity to contemplate one's own mortality. Striking a balance also implies being able to see both sides of an issue, and choosing to see the cup as "half full rather than half empty."

Creativity

Negative thought: "It's hard for me to feel vibrant because I don't get out as much as I used to. The days are so long."

Positive reframe: "This is the time of life I have been waiting for—it allows me to write about my life experiences. There is a well deep inside of me that I have yet to pull from."

As we age, we often can become more creative and open to change. The later years are often accompanied by an enriched sense of self and a greater flexibility. Creativity, like play, can turn us into joyous beings. As we lose ourselves in the process of creativity, we find parts of ourselves that have laid dormant, or have never been expressed.

You may view creativity as it is traditionally expressed: through making an exceptional and concrete item, such as a poem, a painting, a song, or a house, for example. You also may think that creativity is available only to a privileged few. Yet, creativity is a state of mind, an openness to life. It is a term that can be applied to writing a birthday poem, cooking a gourmet meal for a friend, or tackling a routine task in a different manner than before. Creativity involves taking a position in life that allows every act, no matter how routine, to become more important, new, and unusual: "Novelty… has the power to invigorate our minds, our bodies, our hearts and our souls….Doing new things stimulates our brains to grow new dendrites, or connective pathways, which in turn may make it easier for us to take on *more* new things. Doing the same old thing in the same old way…makes our brains…shrivel up and get stale."[24]

Writers Mihaly Csikszentmihalyi[25] and Betty Friedan[26] investigated creativity in their research on aging, although these investigations focused mainly on more traditionally creative, well-known people (artists, musicians, and engineers) who had new ideas in their later years. Still, they shared the following findings. First, they found that artistic or scientific creativity does not uniformly peak in youth. Of those who survive their 40s, many transcended the midlife crisis and developed new directions. A few of the elders who expressed this were William Butler Yeats, Beethoven, and Michelangelo.

Diane S. Schaupp, Ph.D.

According to Friedan, some artists did grow stale for a time, but some returned after a period of stagnation with a more distinct voice: "Why do some artists and scientists keep going on, often after deafness, strokes, or other severe physical impairments? Perhaps because for them the mind (the self) is not impaired in age but continues to grow and to develop."[27] In particular, she was dissatisfied with gerontologists' view on art in later life at the time of the study, commenting, "Why do we feel such a need to diminish or disparage the very possibility of continued creativity in age?" These are difficult questions to answer, but her answer was that "we are locked in a mystique of aging that needs to be researched and broken. For the mystique of aging keeps us locked into the limits of youth so that even gerontologists have not adequately researched creativity in aging."[28]

Csikszentmihalyi interviewed 90 well-known artists, musicians, writers, and engineers to find out how creativity has been a force in their lives. He found that in the humanities and science, the number of contributions held steady between 30 years and 70 years of age, and only in the arts was there a sharp decline after 60. In his sample, respondents did not see much change between their 50s and 70s, or 60s and 80s. They felt that their ability to do work was unimpaired, their goals were substantially the same as they had always been, and the quality and quantity of their accomplishments differed little from what they had been in the past. But, according to Csikszentmihalyi and his respondents, by the time a person moved toward wisdom, a "life well-lived is not so much success but knowing the intimacy of one's being, that our existence is seen in a meaningful way to the rest of the universe."[29]

Now's let's return to a discussion of creativity as it relates to ordinary folks. Focusing on less traditional creative activities can change our life dramatically and broaden our expectations of ourselves. In this sense, creativity isn't easy. Going beyond our daily life and expected activities often requires discipline and the ability to make and meet a challenge. At times, there does not seem to be enough time to think about a new approach to a situation. But, if we can make the time, we can create a unique solution to a difficult situation in our ordinary lives.

The following, from *The Secrets of Becoming a Late Bloomer*,[30] vividly illustrates how a later adult can utilize creativity to sustain body, mind, and spirit.

> Mr. C. was 61 years old when severe arthritis and high blood pressure forced him into making a life changing decision. Up until that time, he had an exciting but stressful career as a foreign correspondent. Mr. C. found that facing death head on gave him a range of choices about living.
>
> He quieted his mind and recognized he wanted to be around animals. He bought a run-down farmhouse on several acres and made plans to retire there.
>
> Slowly, his overall health improved. After about a year, he opened his remodeled fifteen-bedroom farmhouse as a bed and breakfast inn. Many of his old social contacts began to visit his new B & B.

The above is powerful, but you don't have to wait for a major crisis to make creative decisions about the way you want to live. If you take time to reflect, you'll find creative opportunities, large and small, are within your grasp. A creative approach is often easier if you shift your focus from the *product* to the *process*. Sometimes the process results in a product, but not always. That's okay, as the process incorporates a unique and individual way of looking at life, an

Diane S. Schaupp, Ph.D.

attitude that is at once spontaneous, accepting, and non-judgmental.

Because many of you don't think of yourself as creative, chances are you haven't put much energy into developing these more obscure parts of your personality. That's why it's such a challenge to get in touch with your creative impulses and follow them wherever they take you. If you do so, you'll find that what is appropriate for one person may be totally inappropriate for you.

A creative approach to later life celebrates new ways of thinking, feeling, and doing. When you are afraid to create, you are afraid to grow. With a shift in attitude, the way you live a single day can be an adventure. You don't have "to do" to be creative. Daydreaming, watching birds at a feeder, or observing a butterfly at a flower can be a prelude to forms of creativity. Silence and simplicity are food for creative experiences.

Like anything else in life, practice creates progress. If you consciously practice creative acts that fulfill you, you'll develop a closer understanding of the underlying process and appreciate your own abilities more. In later chapters, I will discuss creative techniques, such as journaling, self-talk, and affirmations.

Autumn Harvest

In this chapter, I've covered the inevitable changes that are reflective of the aging process. Hopefully you have begun to shift your view of aging from a dread of growing older to an anticipation of the changes of aging with an increased consciousness and positive attitude. This will help you reach your fullest potential as later adults, and prepare for even later stages of your life such as early and later elderhood.

As a final thought: The only thing that you can count on in life is change, and sometimes changing your *reality* about aging comes from simply changing your *perceptions* about aging. There is an incredible liberation in realizing that you have the power to change your perceptions.

Endnotes

1. Mark H. Beers, Thomas V. Jones, Michael Berkwits, Justin L. Kaplan, and Robert Porter, *The Merck Manual of Health and Aging* (Whitehouse Station, NJ: Merck Research Laboratories, 2004), pp. 788–789.

2. Beers et al., p. 791.

3. Peter Hildebrand, *Beyond Mid-Life Crisis* (London: Sheldon Press, 1995), p. 29.

4. A. Wingfield, L. W. Poon, L. Lombardi, and D. Lowe, "Speed of Processing in Normal Aging: Effects of Speed Rate, Linguistic Structure, and Processing Time," *Journal of Gerontology*, 40 (1985): 579–585.

5. Leonard Hayflick, *How and Why We Age* (New York: Ballantine Books, 1996), pp. 144–145.

6. John Rowe and Robert Kahn, "Human Aging: Usual and Successful," *Science* (July 1987): 61.

7. Rowe and Hahn, p. 61.

8. B. F. Skinner, "Intellectual Self-Management in Old Age," *American Psychologist* 38, (1983): 238–244.

9. Skinner, pp. 238–244.

10. B. A. Wilson & N. Moffat, eds., "Ways to Help Memory," *Clinical Management of Memory Problems*, 2nd ed. (London: Chapman & Hall, 1992), pp. 59–85.

Diane S. Schaupp, Ph.D.

11. B. A. Wilson, Rehabilitation of Memory (New York: Guilford Press, 1987).

12. J. S. Yesavage, J. I. Sheikh, Z. Friedman, and E. Tante, "Learning Mnemonics: Roles of Aging and Subtle Cognitive Impairment," *Psychology of Aging*, 5 (1989): 133–137.

13. Diane Cort-Van Arsdale and Phyllis Newman, Transitions: *A Woman's Guide to Successful Retirement* (New York: Harper and Collins, 1991), pp. 84–126.

14. Ken Dychtwald and Joe Flower, *Age Wave* (New York: Bantam Books, 1990), p. 202.

15. Dychtwald and Flower, pp. 89–98.

16. Melissa Dittman, "A New Face to Retirement," *Monitor on Psychology* 35 (16, November 2004): 78–79.

17. Dittman, pp. 78–79.

18. Nancy Schlossberg, *Retire Smart, Retire Happy: Finding Your True Path in Life* (Washington, DC: American Psychological Association, 2004), pp. 188–213.

19. David Guttman, *Reclaiming Powers* (New York: Basic Books, 1987), p. 203.

20. Robert C. DiGuilio, *Beyond Widowhood: From Bereavement to Emergence and Hope* (New York: Free Press, MacMillan, 1989).

21. Mary Pipher, *Another Country* (New York: Riverhead Books, 1999), p. 275.

22. Pipher, p. 289.

23. George Valliant, *Aging Well* (New York: Little, Brown and Company, 2002), p. 206.

24. Pamela Redmond Satran, "Small Steps to Boost Your Energy," *Ladies Home Journal* (October 2005): 18–22.

25. Mihaly Csikszentmihalyi, *Creativity: Flow and the Psychology of Discovery and Invention* (New York: Harper Collins, 1996), p. 229.

26. Betty Friedan, *The Fountain of Age* (New York: Simon & Schuster, 1993), pp. 121–125.

27. Friedan, pp. 121–125.

28. Csikszentmihalyi, p. 229.

29. Connie Goldman and Richard Mabler, *Secrets of Becoming a Late Bloomer*, New Hampshire: Stillpoint Publishing, 1995), p. 226.

Diane S. Schaupp, Ph.D.

Chapter 9

Growing From Loss

"When we think of loss we think of the loss, through death, of people we love. But, loss is a far more encompassing theme in our life. We experience loss not only through death, but also by leaving and being left, by changing and letting go and moving on."[1] These words were written by Judith Viorst, who was in later adulthood when she wrote *Necessary Losses*. In her book about losses, Viorst spoke about the stark realities we face throughout our life:

that our mother is going to leave us, and we will leave her;

that our mother's love can never be ours alone;

that we are essentially out here on our own;

that we will have to accept—in other people and ourselves—the mingling of love and hate, of good and bad;

that there are flaws in every human connection;

that our status on this planet is implacably impermanent....[2]

Viorst emphasizes in her book that these losses are necessary because we grow by losing and leaving and letting go. In this chapter, I will attempt to help you understand the view that it is only through our losses that we become fully developed human beings. In fact, who we are today is determined by our loss experiences and whether we allow them to overwhelm us. Unpredictable losses and the dreams that we leave behind may lead to growth and the emergence of new competencies.

Letting Go of Dreams

As a result of rising life expectancies and the boomer generation's love of learning and continual personal growth, more and more of us will not only have new dreams in the years ahead, but will follow them. Yet aging also means letting go of dreams and acknowledging that not all of our dreams can be fulfilled. In maturity, we gain the wisdom and skills to get what we want within the limitations imposed by reality—a reality that consists of diminished powers, restricted freedoms, and with people we love, imperfect connections. It includes an acceptance that our dreams that remain unfulfilled are losses. Even so, we can acknowledge our dreams, and use them to express and enjoy what we cannot or dare not live out in everyday life.

The growth that results from acknowledging unfulfilled dreams is that we can assess ourselves and the world with more accuracy. Accepting reality means that we've come to terms with the world's limitations and flaws, as well as our own. It also means establishing achievable goals for ourselves, compromises, and substitutes that we put in the place of our younger selves' aspirations. For example, it takes a lifetime to learn that reality is built of imperfect connections.

Some of us believe that our dreams function as a source of wish fulfillment. They help us satisfy impulses that we

Diane S. Schaupp, Ph.D.

struggle against satisfying in actual life. Through our dreams we satisfy the pleasure and pain of our impulses without having to pay societal consequences. For example, aging women find new sexual vitality once their children leave the home. They may experience fantasies of their own youthful sexuality. For most women they recognize it is not permissible to leave their faithful partners of many years. Rather, they acknowledge the fantasy and find creative outlets in their causes and/or community activities. (We have to exercise caution about allowing our fantasies to serve as substitutes for life. No matter how gratifying our dreams are, we must be able to live with reality and not in our heads alone.)

There are many lost dreams and other losses we are forced to confront in our later years. As pointed out by Judith Viorst earlier in this chapter, losses can be concrete and stark, as in the death of a cherished one, or more abstract, like the loss of a cherished role in our life—a career or our status as a stay-at-home mom, for example. How we handle our losses has a large part in determining the quality of our later years.

Lizzie was the first
to go
suddenly
an aneurysm
of the brain

Elliot
died of AIDS
that fall

Jesse was recruited
to become
a dean
Pryor to run a
family business
in Spokane

Greg left
for reasons too
mysterious
to recall

the rest of us stayed
for another decade

our students changed
no longer quoting Ginsberg
and Kerouac in
peace bands and braids
as in those breathless
early days

Now everyone
is making plans
to leave

Andrew to the
Adirondacks
with his latest
love
Alicia to raise the
Cambodian daughter

Diane S. Schaupp, Ph.D.

she adopted in
mid life

Robert to be with
two young children
and his student wife

Donald makes
commercials on
TV
Beth looks after
grandkids
noon to three

me?
family scattered
no urgent call to
be anywhere
but here
the love affair with
teaching
not quite as potent
but still
alive

I watch my colleagues
disappear
one
by one
to other lives

It's as it's always been

All of us
together
each
alone

on our way home

—Andrea Green, "Finals" [3]

Mourning

We live by losing and leaving and letting go. Eventually, we must accept that loss is inevitable. *Mourning* is the process of adapting to the losses of our life. Throughout a lifetime we pass through changing, perhaps overlapping, phases of mourning. It takes a year or so, sometimes less and sometimes more, for us to pass through a major part of the mourning process.

Dr. Elizabeth Kübler-Ross made a major contribution to our understanding of the mourning process through her work with the dying.[4] She discovered there were stages in the process of acknowledging and coming to terms with death that both dying people and their loved ones needed and wanted to work through. The stages she observed are: Disbelief, Denial, Bargaining, Anger, Depression, Acceptance of the loss, and Moving on.

Starting with shock, and moving through the phases of acute psychic pain, one moves toward what is called "the completion of mourning." "Completion" implies reaching some important degree of recovery, acceptance, and adaptation, but it is important to acknowledge that the loss can be

Diane S. Schaupp, Ph.D.

reconciled from time to time, such as on anniversaries, birthdays, and holidays.

Sometimes we make the dead a part of our inner world, which helps us at last to complete the mourning process. Although important aspects of the relationship are gone, such as sharing a meal or a bed, by making the dead a part of our inner world we will never lose them in some ways. For example, my husband speaks to his father when he notices the tops of the trees sway in the wind. Because of my husband's father's love of nature, my husband sees the swaying of the treetops as a signal that his father is there to listen. A patient of mine thinks about the unconditional love of her mother every time she finds a penny. She does this because her mother used to say to her when she was deep in thought, "A penny for your thoughts."

One form of such internalization is *identification*. Through identification we take into ourselves aspects of those whom we loved and whom are now dead—aspects that are often abstract but on occasion very real. For instance, in my love of nature, I experience the presence of my father and his sister, my favorite aunt, who also loved nature. By taking in the dead—by making them a part of what we think, feel, love, and want to do—we can both keep them with us and let them go.

Yet whether or not sorrow speaks, death may have long-term harmful effects on the mental and physical health of the survivors, who are at a higher rate of passing than those who have not lost someone to death. Studies of stress consistently identify the loss of a close family member as the most stressful event of everyday life. Hundreds of studies show that every life stressor—even those which are minor—increases the risk of mental or physical illness.

Fortunately, not everyone who suffers loss is equally

susceptible to these ills. What decreases a person's vulnerability to loss is:

+ a prior history of good mental and physical health;

+ a spouse who had a satisfying life separate from the marriage;

+ an extended social support system; and

+ age—the older we are, the better we adjust to loss. (Children may mourn a death but not be able to mourn in a way that lets them work through the enormity of the loss. Most need a family of caring adults, so that they can find the necessary support to mourn until they work their way through the process.)

The death of a child is a loss that happens to many. The death of a child is perceived as a death out of season, against the natural order of things. The relationship between a parent and child goes very deep. Anthropologist Geoffrey Gores, in his book, *Death, Grief and Mourning*,[5] concludes that the most distressing and enduring of all grief is a mother's and father's grief for a dead grown child. Mourning the loss of a child, and his or her hopes and dreams, may begin at any stage of the parenting process. Grieving parents may need their loss to be acknowledged and understood by the outside world, as well as by those who experience the loss personally.

In the death of a spouse or a lifelong partner, we mourn our companion, our intimate friend, our protector, our partner in parenthood. We also mourn a way of life: For some of us, the loss of a spouse may be the loss of purpose of our existence; those of us who looked to a spouse for approval may find we also are mourning the loss of that self. "Our society is set up," writes Lynn Caine in her autobiography *Widow*,[6]

Diane S. Schaupp, Ph.D.

"so that most women lose their identities when their husbands die." She says that after her husband's death, "I felt like one of those spiral shells washed up on the beach....No flesh. No life. Whatever lived there is dried up and gone."

The death of a spouse destroys a social unit, imposes new roles, and confronts us—the living—with a terrible loneliness. We may want to hold on to the past but we must mourn the death of our marriage and let it go.

The list of the mourned also includes the loss of a sibling. If the loss occurs in childhood, the loss may be heavily laced with a quiet triumph at getting rid of the rival at last; guilt about the wish to get rid of that rival; and sorrow at being bereft of a playmate. It is a pain of having both won and having lost.

When our brothers and sisters grow up and leave home, some of us establish powerful ties with our siblings that last into adult life; others maintain minimal connections; and others become free as adults to see each other as people and as friends. As time goes by, and parents die and our siblings are all that remain of our first family, we may begin to value our siblings as comrades and co-custodians of our past. We therefore can take their loss exceptionally hard for all these reasons.

The deaths we are supposed to take in stride are the deaths of our parents. But our parents' deaths, as with other losses, have to be mourned. The mourning is sad, but our parents' deaths—especially if they occurred when they were late elders—are part of the natural progression of life. Sometimes our mourning is eased by the thought that our parents died an accepting, peaceful death. Although we miss them, it might have been more difficult if we watched them struggle against death.

In mourning a parent, we also may seek consolation in the thought that we have had a chance to say goodbye—to express our love and gratitude, to finish unfinished business, to achieve some sort of reconciliation. It is said that the loss of parents in the course of adult life can be a growth spurt that pushes new maturity onto us. Similarly, many who have studied mourning maintain that in any kind of death, there is no loss that does not lead to some gain. While most of us would choose to forego the pain and the loss, we are not offered that option. Rabbi Harold Kushner[7] wrote after the loss of his son:

> If I could choose, I would forego all the spiritual growth and depth which has come my way because of ...[my] experiences, and be what I was fifteen years ago, an average rabbi, an indifferent counselor, helping some people and unable to help others, and the father of a bright, happy boy. But, I cannot choose.

Psychoanalyst George Pollock has called the mourning process "one of the more universal forms of adaptation and growth...."[8] Mourning, he says, can lead to creative change, as we can see through the case of Margaret.

Margaret moved forward as a result of her losses, redefining herself in major ways. Many others experience similar shifts in how they view themselves as a result of experiencing loss.

Diane S. Schaupp, Ph.D.

At 67, Margaret now lives alone in the home where she raised her five adopted children. When she was 60, she developed a cancerous tumor that was surgically removed. One morning after Margaret returned from her chemotherapy treatment, her husband went out to walk the dog. The next thing she knew, the police were at the front door of their home. They told her that her husband had been seen collapsing to the ground, and that he had died from a heart attack by the time the medics had arrived.

Margaret wondered if she could endure the pain. She did.

After mourning the loss of her husband, Margaret decided to enroll in college because she had married young and did not graduate. Currently, she is enrolled in a master's of education program. In her free time, she volunteers at a local church teaching English as a second language to migrant workers. She has many friends, both married and single. When her friends ask her if she is interested in meeting someone, her response, to her friends' concern, is that she would rather not: "I want to continue my work helping those less fortunate. I don't know where my work will take me. I don't want to be constrained by a committed relationship."

A Changing Self-Image

As we age, we change, and we begin to mourn the loss of the old image of ourselves. We notice changes in our body and the ways others perceive us. We also notice changes in how we perceive reality, for at several points in our lives we have had to relinquish a former self-image and move on.

Modern research suggests that there are predictable stages

of adult development, where there are periods of stability and periods of transition. In periods of stability, we are putting together a structure for our life—making choices and pursuing goals. In periods of transition, we are challenging the premise of that structure, raising questions, exploring new possibilities. Each transition leads to termination of a previous life structure, and each termination, writes psychologist Daniel Levinson,[8] "is an ending, a process of separation or loss."

As we enter the autumn of life, we start to feel that this is a time of letting go of one thing after another: our waistlines, our vigor, our intention to read all the books we once vowed to read or to go to all the places we once vowed to visit. We even give up on the hope that we will succeed in becoming immortal.

We feel shaken. We feel scared. All of a sudden our friends are having heart attacks. Some have cancer. Some of our friends our age have died. As we acquire new aches and new pains, our health care is being supplied by internists, cardiologists, dermatologists, podiatrists, urologists, periodontists—from whom we want a second opinion. We want a second opinion that will say we are not going to die, at least not right now.

We find that every bodily change and diminished capacity forces us to look at our mortality. When we see declines in our parents, we begin to be faced with our mortality. After they are gone, it will be our turn.

Our children are grown now—our responsibility for them ending—but we are faced with the increasing dependencies of our parents. More and more we find that we are adjusting our life to our parents' dependencies. For many of us, later adulthood is a time when we become our parents' parents. As responsible people, we do the best for them we

Diane S. Schaupp, Ph.D.

can, but admittedly, we like being our children's parents better. Yet, we also find that our children do not need us as much. This is a mixed blessing!

Our past realities are changing. We begin to challenge our self-definition and whether our goals in life hold any value. We begin to sense that the meter of time is running and that our choices are narrowing—that some parts of our life are over forever.

The sense of time running out may serve to facilitate changes in couples' relationships that began in midlife. A male–female shift begins in midlife and continues into later adulthood. Researchers inform us that women become more masculine toward midlife, while midlife men may become less aggressive, less driven to succeed, and in various ways, more "feminine." This change affects the sexual balance and causes relationship tensions, but there also are great advantages to ourselves and to our relationships in unifying the roles in our sexual nature. We can amend our self-definition to include what psychologist Carol Gilligan[10] calls both "voices." In our child-rearing years, we delineate our tasks according to gender, which some think is evolutionary. But as we launch our children, we give up these qualities that we all possess—whether we are woman or man—and we become more fully human.

Another central duality that we confront in midlife and carry into later adulthood is the creative/destructiveness duality. Psychologist Daniel Levinson[11] also addresses man's awareness in midlife of the destructive forces within himself. He writes:

The Mid-Life Transition activates a man's concerns with death and destruction....He becomes more aware of the many ways in which other persons, even loved ones, have acted destructively toward him. What is perhaps worse, he realizes that he has done irrevocably hurtful things to his parents, lovers, wife, children, friends, and rivals. At the same time, he has a strong desire to become more creative, to create products that have value for himself and others, to participate in collective enterprises that advance human welfare, to contribute more fully to the coming generations in society.

In later adulthood; we struggle to unify the opposite tendency of our natures by:

Striving to integrate our feminine self with our masculine self;

Striving to integrate our creative self with the self that knows inner and outer destructiveness;

Striving to integrate a separate self that must be alone with a self that craves connection and, yes, immortality;

Striving to integrate a wiser, later adult self with youthful zest. Our season is autumn, we are preparing for winter. We leave behind our earlier, youthful self-image.

When we relinquish our former unwrinkled and immortal self, we may feel we've done enough; but we're not through.

Ego Transcendence

Our attitude toward our losses as much as the nature of our losses determines the quality of our early and later elderhood. There are women and men who regard every ache and pain, every physical decline, as an intolerable loss. There are those who manage to take a more positive view of the matter.

Diane S. Schaupp, Ph.D.

The difference between these attitudes is the difference, writes social scientist Robert Peck,[12] between "body preoccupation" and "body transcendence," between treating physical aging as our enemy or our master, and making some sort of reasonable peace with it. In her book *Sister Age*, M. F. K. Fisher[13] argues for dealing sensibly with old age by acknowledging and attending to "all the boring symptoms of our ultimate disintegration." But, she also argues that what's important "is that our dispassionate acceptance of attrition be matched by a full use of everything that has happened in all the long wonderful years to free a person's mind from his body…to use experience, both great and evil, so that physical annoyances are surmountable in an alert and even mirthful appreciation of life itself."

Some healthy as well as ill people at age 65 will sink to an old-age self, sentencing themselves to a kind of living death. Some ill as well as healthy people at 80—or until they take their last breath—will live to the hilt.

It is easier to grow old if we have developed a good attitude about what is happening to us and to inevitable losses. When we find ourselves losing some of what we love about ourselves and our lives, we find that a good old age demands a capacity for what we can call "ego transcendence." "Ego transcendence allows us, while perceiving ourselves as finite, to connect to the future through people or through ideas, surpassing our personal limits by means of some legacy we can leave to the next generation. This endeavor to leave a trace is a constructive way of dealing with the grief we are feeling over the loss of self."[14]

Then Comes Our Own Death

Many of us put a great deal of psychological energy into denying death. By this I mean that we go about our lives on a daily basis with our mortality beyond our emotional awareness. In our denial of death, we are able to tolerate the anxiety of our final separation. But there is a cost: Our denial of death consumes a great deal of our psychological energy. The denial of death keeps us from living in the now.

Muriel Spark, a novelist, writes in her book on death, *Memento Mori*: "If I had my life over again, I should form the habit of nightly composing myself to thoughts of death. I would practice, as it were, the remembrance of death. There is no other practice which so intensifies life. Death...should be part of the full expectancy of life. Without an ever-present sense of death life is insipid. You might as well live on whites of eggs."[15]

Most of us find it hard to contemplate our death without being scared of it. In my experience with patients facing death, many have seemed relieved when they are able to share their fears and needs. Edwin Schneidman,[16] who has worked extensively with the dying, writes that there is no set way to achieve grace or other kinds of closure when dying. In fact, Dr. Schneidman says, many people die with loose threads and fragments of life's agenda unfinished.

Are any of us really ready to die? Psychoanalyst Hattie Rosenthal observes in her book, *Psychotherapy for the Dying*, that it "is the person who is convinced that he has lived a full life who is ready to die, and who develops comparatively little anxiety."[17] It seems that the answer to "Are any of us really ready to die?" lies in observing how one lives one's life. For those who value their independence, the inevitable dependencies of death will leave them feeling ashamed. For those

Diane S. Schaupp, Ph.D.

who fear separation, death will fill them with terror. Those who deny reality will continue, until their death, to deny it. But for some, death can provide a new opportunity for growth and change. Dying can precipitate a further stage of emotional development that previously had been beyond our capabilities. K. R. Eissler, in The Psychiatrist and the Dying Patient,[18] writes that "the knowledge or the vague feeling that the end is approaching may enable some people to step aside, so to speak, and view themselves and significant sectors of their lives with humility and also with insight into the futility of so much that is taken too seriously so long as the world is near and man is passionately living in it." Eissler says that a final stage can dissolve certain deeply held ways of being and provides "a last step forward."

He argues that dying can be one of our better achievements in life. He writes:

> "The full awareness of each step that leads closer to death, the unconscious experience of one's own death up to the last second that permits awareness and consciousness, would be the crowning triumph of an individual's life."[19]

For many, a good death is considered a sudden death, such as the death that takes us quietly in our sleep. Contrasted with a slow dying, often alone, in a hospital hooked up to tubes and machines, a sudden death may strike us as a blessing. However, approaching dying as a process with compassionate care and relief from pain may again redefine the good death as one in which there is time to experience our death.

Regardless of whether we have the chance to experience our death, or whether dying becomes a chance for growth, we can enrich our life by remembering that we will die. Yet perhaps we can only do that if we set our death within the context of a life after death.

There is a long history throughout civilization of a need to feel our finite self in the context of something larger that endures. But there are other ways than the spiritual of immortalizing connections and continuities.

For some of us, we live through nature—through trees and rivers and mountains. For others, immortality resides in works and acts that impact future generations. We do not have to appear in history books or be involved in world-changing activities to understand that what we do has an impact on future generations. The image of living on through our children and their children and/or the image of living on through mankind provides a link to the continuity of life from the past to the future, thus providing us with a sense of immortality.

Even though some of us survive with the images of continuity—of immortality—we also live with a sense of transcendence, aware that we don't have the power to prevent our eventual death. Making our way from birth to death, we have learned how to deal with loss....

In confronting losses, we find opportunities for growth. Yes, there is plenty we have to give up to grow. But we cannot love anything without becoming vulnerable to loss.[20]

Endnotes

1. Judith Viorst, *Necessary Losses* (New York: Fawcett Gold Medal, 1987), p. 15.

2. Judith Viorst, p. 16

3. Andrea Green, "Finals," *The Sweet Annie and Sweet Pea Review* 11 (1, 2006): 16–18.

Diane S. Schaupp, Ph.D.

4. Elizabeth Kübler-Ross, *On Death and Dying* (London: Collins-MacMillan, 1969).

5. Geoffrey Gores, *Death, Grief and Mourning* (New York: Doubleday, 1965), pp. 121–126.

6. Lynn Caine, *Widow* (New York: Harper & Row, 1974), p. 1.

7. Harold Kushner, *When Bad Things Happen to Good People* (New York: Schocken Books, 1981), pp. 133–134.

8. George Pollack, "The Mourning Process and Creative Organizational Change," *Journal of American Psychological Association*, 25 (1, 1977): 345.

9. Daniel Levinson, *The Seasons of a Man's Life* (New York: Ballantine Books, 1978), p. 197.

10. Carol Gilligan, *In a Different Voice* (Cambridge, MA: Harvard Press, 1982).

11. Daniel Levinson, p. 197.

12. Robert Peck, "Psychological Developments in the Second Half of Life," in Bernice Neugarten, ed., *Middle Age and Aging* (Chicago and London: The University Press, 1968).

13. M. F. K. Fisher, Sister Age (New York: Alfred S. Knopf, 1983), p. 237.

14. Judith Viorst, pp. 332–333.

15. Muriel Spark, *Memento Mori* (New York: The Modern Library, 1966), p. 149.

16. Edwin Schneidman, *Voices of Death* (New York: Bantam Books), pp. 108–109.

17. Hattie Rosenthal, "Psychotherapy for the Dying," in Hendrick Ruitenbeek, ed., *The Interpretation of Death* (New York: Jason Aronson, 1973), p. 94.

18. K. R. Eissler, *The Psychiatrist and the Dying Patient* (New York: International Press, 1955). p. 318.

19. K. R. Eissler, p. 319.

20. Judith Viorst, p. 377.

Diane S. Schaupp, Ph.D.

Chapter 10
The Graceful You

As we age, we exhibit great courage but we don't appear in the headlines as do our younger counterparts. Yes, our deeds are humbler, and more difficult. Many frail, aging adults model how to face limitations and increasing dependence on others with a grace and dignity that needs to be appreciated.

A New View

We find that as our mobility becomes impaired, we change how we spend our time and conduct our relationships. Few of us will be exempt from the experience of dependency, either through giving or receiving care, and the courage to adjust to these changes tends to be slow and fitful. Depending on others for help can quickly become wearying. Our self-esteem can erode. Regrets about wasted time and unfulfilled dreams may pull at us, causing us to question our priorities around which we previously organized our lives.

As we struggle with each downturn in our being, our

emotions can become increasingly raw. We can strengthen our endurance by learning all that we can about the inner workings of dependency and vulnerability. Eventually, our attitude toward our remaining years and how we will live them will transform, although not until we have reversed our view of ourselves and our understanding of the past.

It Is Better to Give Than Receive

When we give, we are more powerful than when we receive. Giving is the reason that 85-year-old Mary in Chapter 1 was so anxious to return home: "When I am home, I feel independent and in control." At home, Mary has many aging friends who rely on her phone calls. From there she also does a weekly radio show for the visually impaired. Mary does not rely upon her willpower to get up each morning, but rather the necessity of meeting her friends' and radio listeners' need for her help. You see, obligations keep us from wasting ourselves.

Helpers mean well, and doing good deeds for others affirms the self-worth of those helping and the value of their lives. Yet the giving-help–receiving-help relationship is complex, and caregivers often deny opportunities for those who are dependent and vulnerable to give back to counterbalance their dependence. Dependence can be a difficult pill to swallow in a society that values independence, so structuring helping arrangements with the aim of achieving a balanced exchange can make all parties feel better about the relationship.

If your helper refuses consideration or other forms of repayment, the challenge is to learn to receive, because in receiving we are in a more vulnerable position than when we are giving. Yet there are benefits.

Diane S. Schaupp, Ph.D.

Learning to Ask for Help

Being on the receiving side of help is not easy, but through the asking we receive many benefits.

Asking for help reminds us that we are incomplete and needy; that we are to seek outside ourselves to take in what we need. This creates humility, which in turn opens us up to others.

Asking for help means admitting our needs. A transaction between two people occurs when we say, "I have a need. It's not your problem. It's not your responsibility. You don't have to respond. But, I'd like something from you." We are owning that our needs are our responsibility, yet we are allowing others to love us because they truly have something to offer.

By asking for help, we in fact are taking more control of our life—something difficult to see at times. When we ask, we aren't dependent on our friends' ability to read our minds. We are requesting changes in our lives—changes that often are enacted and made. Then, when we are helped, many times we feel grateful, and that gratitude makes us want to help others in turn.

Askers can get more out of relationships through the asking. But if we are seeking emotional connection, asking for a favor will not bring us what we need. The first step of forging a tighter bond with someone therefore might involve saying: "You're important to me, and I'd like to spend more time learning how to be close with you."

Learning to Live With Contradictions

Many of us resist the lessons of helplessness and harden ourselves against the indignities they can provide. We hope for a return to our previous level of functioning and self-sufficiency, and reject the forced revision of priorities our decline offers. We feel bitter about our inevitable dependency and vulnerability; the realization that one morning we will wake up and no one expects our presence or needs our efforts, is startling and unnerving.

We focus on what has been lost, comparing ourselves to others, aspiring for things that are out of reach, and placing blame on something other than what is bothering us deep inside, mainly feelings we thought we got rid of years ago like our dependence and neediness. Watching others adapt to our decline and seeing how our importance in their lives diminishes can sting beyond our capacity for grace.

A wife writes of her ugly emotions toward her slowly deteriorating husband: "The intensity of the anger that hovers there beneath what I take to be love is frightening. I understand the wretched banality of such an anger as this. I do not have to be a professor of whatever to understand the how and the why of such anger, yet it shames and appalls me. And, of course, he knows."[1]

"Why me?" "What can be done?" Our responses to these questions determine our quality of life. Most often we initially respond to "Why me?" with anger and "What can be done?" with despair. It is easy to lose the hope that we will cope, but eventually we must pull ourselves away from what has been lost. Fear cannot be swept away, but we have to focus in a new direction.

Yet no sooner do we become accustomed to a new condition than another imposes itself. We swing from gratitude to

Diane S. Schaupp, Ph.D.

bitterness, and back again. We have to keep devising satisfactions, and then releasing our hold on them. The choices we must make are constant. We either open ourselves to new consolations, or bitterness prevails.

How do we stay on the open road? The route to personal adaptability begins with old strengths. We're carried by patterns back to ourselves. In Anatomy of an Illness, Norman Cousins describes visiting Pablo Casals when the master cellist was 89:

> He arranged himself with some difficulty on the piano bench. Then with discernable effort raised his swollen and clenched fingers above the keyboard....His back straightened. He seemed to breathe more freely....Then he plunged into a Brahms concerto and his fingers, more agile and powerful, raced across the keyboard with dazzling speed. His entire body seemed fused with the music; it was no longer stiff and shrunken but supple and graceful and completely freed of its arthritic coils.[2]

We have to exert a deliberate effort, day by day, to make life as good as the body allows. We must realize the value of each of our retained abilities and each new capacity we have acquired. We have to remain focused on this, or discouragement prevails.

Aging humbles us and makes more of us at the same time. When our primitive needs move to the forefront of daily life, we are put in touch with parts of ourselves that have lain dormant for years. We are fortunate that with the inevitable losses of aging, we no longer have to cling to previous patterns and strivings toward independence that society has forced upon us.

Wanting both to be helped and left alone, to have

allowances made and to be treated normally, those who feel vulnerable may push help away at the same time that they hope others will find ways to make life easier for them. In listening with the "third ear," the analyst Theodore Reik points out that such dividedness is not a problem to be solved, but rather an aspect of the human condition that must be accepted: "Opposite tendencies can coexist in us, feelings contradicting each other live together, and what is true and what is false can be confused....So much lives in us —wishes and their denials, faith and mistrust, appetites and distastes. They change places so frequently that what is fair becomes foul and what is foul, fair."[3]

The more independence we lose, the more torn we become by contradictory urges. Asking for help is complicated and can evoke a multitude of conflicted emotions. Impatience with explaining, revealing, and excusing oneself results, when what one really wants is that people would know what to do and would simply do it without having to be asked or reminded. When a helper can get things done without announcing or making a show of his or her efforts, it does not take away the pride of the vulnerable person being helped.

Until a compromise is reached that allows for both self-assertion and collaboration, those who are vulnerable often struggle over a confusing pendulum of contradictions. They are never sure how much leaning on others is acceptable and how much effort they should exert in their attempts to overcome obstacles and frustrations.

Diane S. Schaupp, Ph.D.

Interdependence for Survival

No matter what our previous attitudes were about independence, if we want to age well, we have to face our need for attachment to others throughout the lifespan. The attachments we form matter more than anything else at the end.

In *Counting on Kindness*, Wendy Lustbader explains: "If we conducted the middle of our lives with an eye to the end of our lives, we would choose a place to live and we would stay. Residing near others with whom we establish a history of reciprocity is the best hope for old age, whether we manage to live near blood relations or choose to develop family-like bonds with others."[4]

As life gets physically more challenging, we need commitment to others to bind us to life. Many people surprise themselves with the quality of friendships they are able to form. Arlie Hackschild in *The Unexpected Community* portrays her observations of the relationships between residents in a senior apartment complex. She describes a sibling-like equality and reciprocity, stating, "some periods of life, such as adolescence and old age…an individual is open to, and needs, these back-up relationships."[5]

In *The Evolving Self*, Robert Kegan counters the view that more independence is a sign of progress in life by suggesting that we all experience a lifelong yearning for "integration, attachment, inclusion."[6] He maintains that this need develops in tandem with the urge for autonomy, no matter how we try to suppress or ignore it.

Slowing Down

Aging may disrupt so many of the patterns that constrained us that only in old age may we at last attain the freedom to be fully ourselves. Many of the crises of later life are marked by attempts to retain old patterns of satisfaction, but it is only when we let go of the familiar that fresh life can come in and revive us.

As we age, we lose physical vitality. When life slows down in so many ways, it returns the open time and emotional spaciousness of childhood to us. We are especially free to engage in worlds of our own making. In "The Life Review: An Interpretation of Reminiscence in the Ages," Robert Butler writes, "Probably not in another time of life is there as potent a force toward self-awareness operating as in old age."[7] Taking back our earlier yearnings, or daring to develop them for the first time, is one of the key privileges of having time on our hands. Playing music for the pleasure of it, learning to dance for the sensation of it, or painting for the adventure of it, are the kind of activities that we may abandon to our detriment during our middle years.

People who experience agelessness in their manner of living have learned to be content, to cultivate and make the best of their world. In *Growing Young*, Ashley Montagu celebrates the finalities of open-mindedness, personal adaptability, a sense of wonder, and enthusiasm as "the most valuable possessions of our species, to be cherished, nurtured and cultivated."[8] The intrusion of death in our affairs has proven to us that it is enough to go on living and to take pleasure where we can find it.

Diane S. Schaupp, Ph.D.

Acts of Compassion

Content living signals we have begun to live life in terms of, rather than in flight from, the approach of our ending. In *The Experience of Nothingness*, Michael Novak writes, "The drive to question allows the human animal to lift his eyes from the sequence of daily routines to perceive the law of his own death, and to struggle for ways of life that assuage death's bitterness."[9] After such experiences, changes may emerge in the way we spend our time, conduct our relationships, and look to the future.

But, why do some of us develop compassion? Compassion may not be explainable in rational terms. Compassion is most moving when it is rendered in the absence of something to gain. One person notices the difficulty of another, and acts accordingly. In *The Possibility of Altruism*, Thomas Nagel writes, "It is a question not of compassion but of simply connecting in order to see what one's attitudes commit one to. Recognition of the other person's reality and the possibility of putting yourself in his place is essential."[10]

In my clinical practice, I have observed that people who value others tend to carry these inclinations with them to the end of their lives. Wherever they live, whatever they do, they readily make connections with other people and derive satisfaction from doing so. Then, when vulnerability encroaches, they tend to be surrounded by caring helpers.

The belief that there will be people around us in our time of need is a conviction that we create by our example: We see firsthand that individual efforts can indeed reduce suffering, and we suspect that the measure of life is how we are treated at the end.

Not all hardships are beyond human control. We hope

that if we become incapacitated, our familial relatives will stand by us, as we have stood by them and/or others.

Self-Care

Success in dealing with whatever hand we are dealt is learning how to take good care of ourselves emotionally, physically, and spiritually. Living a healthy lifestyle helps us learn how to care for ourselves. It is an art that is the backbone of any kind of renewal.

The first key to success in self-care involves being conscious of, and expressing adequately, our feelings.

Expressing All of Your Feelings

For some, simply the idea of expressing personal feelings leads to feelings of embarrassment and vulnerability. They bury their feelings so frequently that this has become part of their daily routine. The tin woodsman character in Frank L. Baum's *Wizard of Oz*[11] represents the part of us that's cut off from our feelings.

When Dorothy found the rusted tin woodsman, she ran for an oil can and gave him a good squirt. When the tin woodsman could talk, he told Dorothy that he had once been a real person with a real body, in love with a young woman he planned to marry. But The Witch of the East cut away his entire body and replaced it with tin. He was no longer covered in warm flesh, but trapped in unfeeling armor.

This story can happen to us. When we suppress our feelings, we become disconnected from how we really feel and from the passionate voice of our heart. Such a split between

Diane S. Schaupp, Ph.D.

heart and head is common in our culture.

As we separate from our feelings, we tend to separate from our bodies as well. When we suppress feelings, we lose energy. It may save us from pain, but it diminishes our ability to feel alive.

The antidote is to try to be open to your feelings. Experiencing feelings is the first step toward making yourself known not only to oneself but to others. After you imagine a feeling, describe the feeling and learn to express it appropriately. Buried feelings fester and form anger, depression, and illness. We have to move through the more negative feelings to be able to move to more positive ones.

Here are some thoughts on how to deal with negative or dispiriting emotions as they are brought more into your conscious awareness.

Grappling with Grief and Sadness

It is not possible to go through life without having incredibly sad things happen to us. At these times, we must walk through the grieving process, not around it, to get to the light. Grieving is normal and necessary in order to get on with life.

We are who we are in part because of the people in our life. The closer we are to another, the more our own self and self-image are tied to them. The loss we experience when someone close to us dies involves not only that person, but the part of us that is complexly intertwined with that person. A part of us dies with that person. When that person dies, it is time for us to redefine ourselves without that person.

Grieving involves work to reclaim that part of our self that is lost. It is important to realize that there is a scar, and a part of us is changed forever. Events and memories can trigger a reopening of the loss throughout our life.

There isn't a right way to grieve. Those who short-circuit their grieving don't allow themselves to express their feelings fully. Short-circuiting the grieving process impedes our ability to preserve the person we lost within us or release the person from within if that is what we need to do for our emotional growth.

Anger

Anger has many aliases such as frustration, apathy, hurt, sorrow, and disappointment. It is an emotion that people often are unable to express well.

Often we get the message that anger is not okay. Feelings are not right or wrong; they just are. A trait of a mature person is the ability to express anger in a mature way. It is best to express anger as you feel it rather than suppress it, as the energy cycle is as follows:

1. You become aware of feelings of anger because of unmet expectations, abuse, or loss of respect for yourself or others. You also might feel anxious, disappointed, uncomfortable, or powerless.

2. You feel an energy buildup.

3. Relief comes only after expression of the feeling.

When you do not express anger directly, you experience:

+ *Depression*: Unexpressed anger turned inward manifests itself as depression. Depression leaves us feeling emotionally flat and withdrawn.

+ *Physical Symptoms*: Unexpressed anger can manifest

itself in tension, headaches, stiff necks, high blood pressure, diminished sexual desire, lower back pain, and lowering of the autoimmune system.

✢ *Anger Explosions*: Angry explosions result from a buildup of anger, which erupts disproportionately to the triggering event. Explosions scare people away and inhibit good communication.

✢ *Passive-Aggressive Behavior*: Passive-aggressiveness can take the form of cutting sarcasm, inappropriate humor, or hostile remarks. Because the anger is expressed indirectly, it is hard to pick up, but if recipients have been hurt, unconsciously their tendency is to stay away from you.

A healthy assertion of anger is possible if you keep the tips that follow in mind:

✢ *Be specific about what is bothering you*: "You aren't paying attention to me."

✢ *Use "I" messages when expressing yourself*: "I feel insignificant and alone when you do that."

✢ *Ask for a different behavior*: "If we planned to do more together, I would care more."

✢ *Point out the outcome you anticipate*: "I think we'd both feel closer and our relationship would change."

Sometimes, however, what makes us uncomfortable is not our own expression of anger but being on the receiving end of anger. We are unsure what to do, and the extremity of the emotion being expressed may make us uncomfortable. Here are a few easy ways to respond to people's anger in a way that makes us more comfortable with its expression:

✢ Practice active listening: "You sound hurt. This really means a lot to you." The other person will enjoy having a sounding board, and being heard starts to calm them down.

✛ Take a time-out: "I am going to take a walk around the block. I'll be back shortly and will see if we are ready to talk more about this." Taking a time-out is a great way to hold the emotions until both parties are ready to discuss them in a calm fashion.

Completing Unfinished Business

Many times in life there are situations from our past that need resolution. Holding on to resentments against another can have a negative impact on us, for it is only when we decide that resentment is not worth the toll it is taking on us that we can move on.

It does require two people to release the tension and antagonism that blocks completion. When we can open our heart, feel the pain, and release it and all the energy it holds, we begin to move toward greater inner healing and peace.

This kind of change can happen in many different ways. Some people ritualize the process: They set the stage by arranging a special place, gathering together memorabilia and music symbolic of the person or situation. Or they go to a favorite place in nature and stretch out in a meadow, etc., where they begin an imaginary dialogue with the person with whom they have unfinished business. I suggest using one of the following meditations for letting go:

For another: "I ask you (name) for forgiveness. Please free me."

For self: "I forgive myself for any past unknowings and deeds, those that were intentional or unintentional. I want to love and care for myself and be new and free."

For another: "I let go of the pain and hurt that I have felt in this relationship. It prevents me from living my life fully in the present. I no longer want to waste my energy or to allow these feelings to have power over me."

It is important to remember that we receive the personal benefits of inner healing and peace through forgiveness.

Maintaining a Healthy Lifestyle

Health habits greatly affect how we age. Physical fitness doesn't necessarily lengthen our life, but it improves the quality of life because we feel better. The focus of this book is more on the emotional aspects of aging, but the importance of how we take care of ourselves physically cannot be separated out. Staying attuned to our bodies is as important as staying attuned to ourselves emotionally and spiritually.

Sustaining Grace from Day to Day

To maintain a graceful aging day by day, it helps to ponder the following questions on a regular basis so that you sustain and strengthen your personal adaptability:

+ What positive attitudes do I want to repeat tomorrow?

+ Have I responded to my mistakes appropriately? If not, what would I do differently?

+ Have I responded to others with empathy?

Nurturing such personal adaptability is a lifelong, open-ended process that is constantly changing. Assessing our progress periodically is necessary to respond effectively to the inevitable changes that aging brings.

If you are interested in finding out more about how to bring more meaning to your life, turn to the next chapter. There I discuss the spiritual side of clarifying your values and learning to find quality in your journey as you age.

Endnotes

1. Martha Weinman Lear, *Heartsounds* (New York: Pocket Books, 1980), p. 379.

2. Norman Cousins, *Anatomy of an Illness as Perceived by the Patient* (New York: Bantam Books, 1981), pp. 72–73.

3. Theodore Reik, *Listening with the Third Ear: The Inner Experience of a Psychoanalyst* (New York: Farrar, Strauss and Giroux, 1983), p. 173.

4. Wendy Lustbader, *Counting on Kindness* (New York: The Free Press, 1991), p. 132.

5. Arlie Russell Hachschild, *The Unexpected Community: Portrait of an Old Age Subculture* (Berkeley: University of California, 1978), pp.70, 72.

6. Robert Kegan, *The Evolving Self: Problems and Process in Human Development.* (Cambridge, MA: Harvard University Press, 1982), pp. 107–108.

7. Robert Butler, "The Life Review: An Interpretation of Reminiscence in the Aged," in Patrick L. McKee, ed., *Philosophical Foundations of Gerontology* (New York: Human Sciences Press, 1982), p. 238.

8. Ashley Montagu, *Growing Young* (Granby, MA: Bergen and Garvey Publishers, 1989), p. 175.

9. Michael Novak, *The Experience of Nothingness* (New York: Harper & Row, 1978), p. 48.

10. Thomas Nagel, *The Possibility of Altruism* (Princeton, NJ: Princeton University Press, 1970), p. 83.

11. Frank L. Baum, *The Wizard of Oz* (New York: Henry Halt, 1942), pp. 41–44.

PART IV

THE LIFE YOU CAN CREATE

Chapter 11

Accepting Our Humanity: This Is How I Want to Live My Life

What does it mean to live life fully and meaningfully? Living fully means keeping one's heart open—to ourselves, to others, to life itself with all of its ups and downs. Yes, that's right—its "ups and downs." Living fully does not mean that we will be problem free or without some pain. Caring about others gives us pain…and yet caring is also the best way for us to heal when we hurt. Healing is choosing to move toward love and kindness versus closing ourselves off and resisting life.

It's a paradox that if we love and care about anyone or anything, we are guaranteed a certain amount of pain. But one of the criteria for enlightenment and living life fully is to accept the inevitability and cyclical nature of grief. It is when we back away from caring to protect ourselves from pain that we lose the joy of truly living.

To live meaningfully, we need to know that we have made a difference to someone or something. People's souls are hungry for meaning, even though it isn't possible to find ultimate meaning. We can find, however, little clarifying meanings that move us in the direction of ultimate meaning. As we seek ultimate meaning, we will be given opportunities to act in a meaningful way.

Experience can bring wisdom, but does not necessarily. It is what we learn from our experiences that brings wisdom. Having additional years of experience offers us possibilities of clarity about events that were previously incomprehensible, and provides a chance of seeing how our journey fits into the bigger picture.

As we reach later adulthood, we want more than ever a life that has mattered and continues to matter. By now, we have learned that it is not material acquisitions or power that satiates our hunger. When our life has meaning we feel happy; happiness is the by-product, not the goal.

Those who have a goal and look for meaning exude purposefulness whether or not their physical body is cooperating. I'm sure you know people whose ailing bodies dominate their every moment. In other words, some of us treat our aging body as our enemy and focus on it so obsessively that aging becomes the master. Then there are the others who find meaning beyond themselves.

Author Gail Sheehy writes, "At some point in our 50s or 60s, most of us will face a crisis of great magnitude, such as when a serious illness strikes us or our partner....Dramatic life accidents such as these strip away the edifice of our well-defined lives, and a hunger wells up for a greater depth of meaning and value in the activities of our everyday lives."[1]

It's important not to allow your body and any increasing limitations to dominate your life. Find meaning by clarifying what's important to you and making everyday behaviors consistent with your values.

The circle of life begins to close when we determine what

Diane S. Schaupp, Ph.D.

provides meaning to our lives. As you move through this chapter, you will become more aware of what that is for you. You also will discover practical ways to document what is important to you. As you continue on this journey, you will understand yourself better and see how your journey connects you to others.

Value Clarification

Our values are our foundation. They determine what we need to be fulfilled. When our actions are not congruent with our values, we feel pulled in incompatible directions. Over time, this sort of stress depletes our emotional resources, which we need to handle life's inevitable losses.

Values are a valuable resource. When we feel confused, we can turn to them for self-definition; in times of trouble, they give us strength. We experience emotions, but our values help determine thoughtful actions on our part. When we make a determination to take an action that represents our values rather than our emotions, we feel inspired.

If we aren't living in congruence to our values, we are more vulnerable to stress. The only way out of this vulnerability is to clarify what we really care about and to work on expressing these values in the way we live our life. Living a meaningful life with conviction is the best way to turn stress out of our life.

Our feelings need validation. Once we validate our feelings, we can determine an action that is congruent with our values.

So many times we move blindly through life without considering what is valuable to us. Complete the following questionnaire to help you gain an understanding of those things you hold the most dear.

1. Which four things do I want most in my life?
(Prioritize your answers, with 1 being the most valuable
to you.)

_____eternal life

_____global peace

_____preservation of the environment

_____civil rights

_____personal accomplishments

_____emotional/sexual intimacy

_____Living for others

_____economic security

_____inner peace

_____good health

_____freedom of choice

_____wisdom

_____stimulation

_____recognition

_____self-respect

_____other choice(s) (specify)

2. What would I like to appear on my tombstone?

_____

_____

3. What would I like to say before I die? _____

_____

Diane S. Schaupp, Ph.D.

4. What would people say about me after I die?_____

_____

5. Whom do I love? What qualities do I love most about them?_____

_____

_____

_____

_____

6. When have I felt most alive? (Write briefly about each of these times.)_____

_____

_____

_____

7. What are my most important values at this moment?

_____

_____

To test the congruence of your personal values with your daily life, consider what you are doing to express your most important personal values in your relationships, your health, and your life's work. For instance, if you value emotional intimacy, your life might look like the following:

Relationships: Communicating consistently with family and friends; feeling a sense of goodness; assuming a basic trust in people.

Health: Taking care of myself by exercising, getting enough sleep, eating right, and managing my emotions in the face of stress.

Life Work: Taking care of myself so I can help others'

personal growth (i.e., using the airplane concept—"use oxygen for yourself first, so you will be strong enough to administer to others").

Now fill out the following areas yourself:

Relationships:_____
_____
_____
_____

Health:_____
_____
_____
_____

Lifework:_____
_____
_____
_____

Next, ask yourself if you are doing all that you can to keep your personal values and daily life congruent. If there are discrepancies, problem solve how you can align your life with your personal values.

When setting up ways to change the unaligned areas, set up a plan with concrete steps so you can picture each step clearly enough to decide whether you want to give it a try. Here's an example.

Relationships: I consider my immediate family to be the No. 1 priority in my life, but I don't get to see my son that much. We don't have much in common these days anyhow. I also haven't been in touch much with the grandkids since my son's divorce.

Solution: I'm going to resolve to fly out to see my son twice a year, even though I don't like getting on a plane. Because my grandchildren now live with their mother most of the time, I will get a cell phone and learn how to send them text messages—I know they love modern technology. I'll also try to call them once a week, when they're at their father's house. All this should help me in talking with my son: I'll now know more about what his children are up to. He misses seeing them on a daily basis, so he'll enjoy being able to talk more about them with me.

Now it's your turn to problem solve. If you find you're a little short on answers in some areas right now, don't be too hard on yourself; life has its constraints. Change is a step-by-step process, and it can be slow going at times.

Take Nancy as an example. Her goal to find a more meaningful path began with discussing her needs with her husband. The changes she wanted to make, such as moving from where they lived, were considerable, so at each step of the change she was making, she asked herself whether the losses from these changes would be offset by the gains, thus making her life more meaningful. If they weren't, she reconsidered the change(s).

As you begin to envision and lay out the changes you want to make in those areas with which you are struggling, ask yourself whether these changes will live up to your personal values. If they will, you'll begin to recognize your real strengths in life and you'll get excited. This will generate energy for the change process.

When considering what to change, look at the areas that are reflecting success at living your personal values. Then look at those that aren't: Can you learn more about how to improve the areas in which you aren't living close to your personal values? Ask yourself why not: "Did I not put a high priority on this?" "Did I not have the right support system?" Use your life successes as a blueprint to see what is truly possible.

The idea is not to fix everything all at once. An old Chinese proverb says that the journey of a thousand miles begins with a single step. Keep in mind where you are right now and a vision of where you want to go. That is how a life is well lived.

It's All About Quality

Our quality of life is *our* perception of what is meaningful to us and the reality of the situation. Our perception changes as we are introduced to new events and new interests. Quality of life is not static, which is why it is important to rethink what is meaningful to us: What makes us feel good about ourselves? How much time do we spend doing things we enjoy and value? What can we change to improve our quality of life? Are our relationships supporting our values?

It is important to let people know how strongly we feel about things. As we age, we become more reliant on others to help us with some of our needs. We can't expect others to know what we need if we don't explicitly tell them what we like and what we don't like. Learning how to ask for what we want and to be a receiver of help may be one of our hardest lessons and one of the most important behaviors to model.

Reaching age 60, we automatically rethink what is important: "Will I continue to work? If not, what would I like to do with my time?" But in early elderhood, other important

Diane S. Schaupp, Ph.D.

quality of life issues are eminent, such as living arrangements: "Would I prefer to remain in my own house, move to an apartment, move in with a family member who would then become a caregiver, or move to a facility that provides more care?"

We also begin to think about what directives we will leave behind when someone else is responsible for us. The decisions we make reflect our personal values and what has been important to us. For example, do you want life supports discontinued if it has been medically determined that you have irreversible brain damage? Or, if your doctor determines that you have the early symptoms of Alzheimer's, do you want to know? On any given day in newspapers, there are examples of the ethical dilemmas we will face. It is difficult to approach and get in the habit of discussing such emotionally intense matters, but it is important to let your views be known to those who may make decisions for you.

Taking Control by Leaving Directives

Today we have a chance to plan and claim responsibility for those things in life that directly affect the quality and extent of our physical lives. This also is a chance to let people know what is important to us. This section gives background information on options and defines relevant terms such as living wills and durable power of attorney for health care.

Taking control of this aspect of your life gives you the gratifying feeling of knowing that you have done all you can to make your life as personally satisfying as possible until the very end. It also relieves your family members from the prospect of burdensome responsibility and confusion.

Living Wills

A living will is a written statement, signed by you and witnesses, which gives guidance to your family and doctor about your health care wishes in preparation for a time when you might not be able to make decisions for yourself. It is sometimes referred to as an *advanced directive for health care*. You can state whether you do or do not want to undergo particular life-prolonging medical procedures if your condition is considered irreversible and terminal. It is important to note that in many states, a living will only goes into effect when you are in a terminal condition. (*The durable power of attorney for health*, discussed next, is activated if you are either in a nonterminal or terminal condition in which you are unable to make or communicate your health care wishes.)

Each state has legislated guidelines for advanced directives, and while specific provisions vary from state to state, they all authorize a competent adult to execute a declaration in advance about his or her health care preferences.

A proxy decision maker also can be named in many states' living will forms. This designated proxy will make medical decisions on your behalf if you become unable to make them for yourself. The living will document provides a vehicle to ensure that those decisions are made in accordance with your preferences and, because those preferences are written out for all to see, the surrogate decision maker need feel no remorse over carrying out your wishes.

It is important to know that a living will can be changed at any time. Situations change. Living situations, health, and even relationships change, warranting an update of living wills.

When there is a question of a person's competency to make decisions about their health care, an attending physician, a psychologist, or a neurologist may be hired to determine a person's capacity to make health care decisions. Legally, a person is considered competent to make a treatment decision if he or she has the ability to understand relevant information about the medical problem and the consequences of the decisions about treatment. To determine whether a person is able to make decisions, it is important for families to ask whether the person is making decisions consistent with underlying values previously expressed, and whether the choices being made promote the individual's well-being.

Living will forms vary from state to state. The organization Partnership in Caring will provide you with a state-specific form and information if you go to their Web site http://www.partnershipforcaring.org or call 1-800-989-WILL (9455).

The nonprofit Aging with Dignity, Inc. (http://www.agingwithdignity.org or 888-594-7437), provides living will documents for a small fee (as of this writing, $5.00); the National Hospice and Palliative Care Organization (http://www.nhpco.org or 703- 837-1500) gives away such forms for free.

Once you have drafted your living will, provide copies for your doctor, proxy (competent person), family, clergy, lawyer, and anyone else close to you.

Discussing your living will with others will help them understand your wishes better. Such a discussion also will give your family and physician the chance to ask any questions they might have and let them know whether they are comfortable following your wishes. The major value of the living will is the discussion itself—letting others know what you think about critical care issues.

Some of the critical issues to think about, and specify

your wishes in regard to, are cardiac resuscitation, radiation, dialysis, antibiotics, respirator treatment, chemotherapy, and artificial feeding and hydration. Because we cannot know the details about how we will eventually die, it is good if our doctor and surrogate understands our general views, so that they are then able to apply them to decisions that have to be made at the appropriate time. The nonprofit group www.medicaldirective.org will offer documents for $15 as well as detailed work sheets describing possible medical situations for patients and families to consider.

Durable Power of Attorney for Health Care

The durable power of attorney for health care (DPAHC) is a legal document written for the purpose of designating another person to make health-related decisions on our behalf if our attending physician feels we are unable to do so for ourselves. This document is comparable to the proxy designation of a living will, and is preferable to the living will if your state does not provide the opportunity for proxy designation. Unlike the living will, which in many states applies only when the patient is deemed *terminal*, the DPAHC enables the designated agent to make decisions if we are temporarily, or permanently, unable to make decision(s). Some states have durable power of attorney that applies only to property matters; in others, the advance directives for health care document both property and health care matters.

Make sure you know what you want to accomplish with a DPAHC, and be as specific as possible. This could include enabling access to medical information and records; employing and discharging medical personnel; refusing consent for specific procedures; requesting pain relief; or arranging for care and lodging in a hospital, nursing home, or hospice. It

　　　　Diane S. Schaupp, Ph.D.

is especially important to specify in writing wishes about artificial food and hydration.

Also, make sure that you clearly inform your health care agent of your values and wishes.

It Is My Responsibility

If you have chosen to fill out an advanced directive, you are well on the way to enjoying that peace of mind that comes from knowing that you have done what you can to take control of your needs in the future. You are maintaining responsibility for *you*.

The best way to flourish in your later years is to take responsibility for your life and make both informal and formal choices. There are many ways that you can plan for this time of life, but the fundamentals are relatively constant. First, you need to obtain current information on subjects that interest you. Second, you need to clarify what your feelings and values are, and make choices that are congruent with them. Third, you need to communicate, informally, that awareness to those close to you, and formally, ways that further guarantee your wishes will be carried out. People feel best about themselves when they know that they have choices and that they have responsibly put things in order. They then can comfortably focus on how they want to live their later years, and go about doing so.

How to Make Life Meaningful

When you retire, whether it is in your 60s or 80s, it can be a time when you may feel like a boat trying to cross the Atlantic Ocean without a rudder or a compass. One question we can ask is, "Who am I? What should I be doing today?" For years, we wanted more time to choose to do other things, but our lives were organized around a different area—our career maybe, or our children. With our latter years lacking that organizational structure, we are faced with a dilemma of not knowing what we are going to do each day. We are faced with the questions of how to manage all the time we have on our hands and too many choices.

The dilemma you are facing is the result of a new stage of life that you are transitioning into. You might need to return to Chapter 4 to refresh your memory about developmental transitions. How you decide to spend your time and how much time you will spend doing it will be determined by your personal values. There will be some activities that you have always loved to do but you never had enough time to do them. Do them now. Then there will be those activities that are completely new and different. Allow your curiosity to guide you. Remember, giving up some of the "old you" to make room for the "new you" can feel uncomfortable. Remain confident that this discomfort will pass as you explore new options.

What new things do you want to try? As you take in what you learned about your values earlier, consider what activities would make you feel good about yourself. Is it time to do some of the things you regret not having done earlier in life? Maybe some of the changes you want to make are internal. If you spent too much of your life trying to please others, maybe you will decide to focus more on what would please you. Others might like to make external changes. What would you like to try now that you were unable to do in the past because of your previous commitments?

Here are examples of ways some later adults have chosen to make their lives meaningful:

Help Others: Volunteer to help with a project such as Habitat for Humanity that connects you to the welfare of others. Commit random acts of kindness and senseless acts of beauty. Create meaning by saying "Hello" to others or writing friendly notes to people.

Find a New Job: Predictions are that many will experience several careers in their lifetime. I am working toward adding the career of author to my resume as I move through later adulthood to early elderhood.

Try Something New: Whether it be singing, dancing, traveling, trying new recipes, pottery, or jewelry making, do something you have always thought about but never had time to do.

Teach Others New Skills: Whether it is teaching a grandchild to bake or volunteering to help people manage their money better, volunteering helps to keep the focus outside of ourselves and provides relief from aches and pains.

Develop New Hobbies: Try golfing or fishing, bird watching or antique collecting.

Prepare To Pass Down Family History: You can be the link that preserves your next generation's connection to their past.

You, yes you, can participate in the new movement to change the negative stereotypes of aging adults by modeling a full life, by being a person who enjoys the benefits your stage of life brings. If you model the empowerment that can come with later life by continuing to learn, risk, care about things, and be joyful, it will help change the outdated image of aging.

Living Each Moment

One of the experiences we can have as we age is to enjoy the moment. By enjoying the moment, we have learned to make after 60 a prime time of life. Most of us do not have the lifestyles we had in middle age—the rushing that kept us from noticing life's small pleasures. Not only do we have perspective as a result of our years of experience, but we also have leisure time and an awareness of our mortality that helps us appreciate simple pleasures.

In this book, you have been learning the value of living in "autumn" rather than accepting the standards of "summer." What does living in the autumn mean? Instead of emphasizing "doing," we're learning to balance "doing" with "being." Rather than "making it," we are focusing our psychological energy on adjusting to losses and health issues. Facing our mortality brings a greater appreciation of living.

We're also trading off concerns about the future, becoming more present in "the now," and living more spontaneously. By learning to live in autumn, we are learning to tolerate uncertainty and living lightheartedly. We are no longer willing to let society set our agenda; we are making our own. Humility is setting in, and we are okay with not having answers. We no longer live by what we "have to" do. We do what we want to do.

We move our focus from our immediate world to seeing ourselves as part of a greater whole. We also are beginning to balance our need for control and independence with a freeing ability to "let go." We are able to accept our accomplishments with gratitude, and accept what we couldn't accomplish. At the same time, our inner work is more important.

To find life meaningful, it is important for us as we age to see these stages of life as valuable as the earlier years. All stages of life have gains and losses, and this time of life is full of opportunities for meaning and satisfaction. As you continue to consider what is meaningful, ponder what moments in your life so far have been the most meaningful to you.

For some of us, those cherished moments are when we feel fully known by another. They have occurred when we watched our child being born, when we felt awed by the magnificence of nature, or when we talked to someone about how we really felt about something and we felt accepted. These moments are an integral part of us. They are points in time that touched us deeply, times when we felt one with the universe. By remembering these moments, we will begin to understand what makes us feel most alive. Following our bliss means that we actively pursue such moments as we continue to live. When we realize what makes us feel most alive, we can use this awareness as a source of guidance.

In knowing what makes us feel most alive, we can begin to direct our journey. While a graduate student, I knew that jumping through endless hoops would enable me to contribute in a way that would give my life meaning in the long run. I write this because I know that to actively follow one's bliss is not always easy, but when it is our choice, the struggles are transformed into meaningful moments, like the satisfaction I feel when someone leaves my office with a fuller grasp of how he or she wants to live life.

As we age, we have to find new ways to follow our bliss. When in a wheelchair or bedridden, what gives our life meaning may be different. Bliss is not necessarily an activity.

It could be listening to a nurse's aide as she describes her struggles with an adolescent son or daughter, or watching a new bird feed at our feeder.

The Japanese tea ceremony is an example of making trivial seeming acts vital. During the tea ceremony, attention focuses on the present as the subtle details of the occasion are noticed: the taste of the tea; the aroma of the incense; the sound of the whisk as it blends the green tea powder into a frothy brew. In the tearoom, no one wears a watch. Nothing is discussed except what pertains directly to the tea experience. According to the Japanese, the timeless presence of the tea ceremony extends itself beyond the tearoom into life.

Considering simplicity from a developmental perspective, we move from the spontaneous experience of joy as a youngster to that of a focus on complexity in middle age, and then we move back to appreciate simplicity as we age. Our later life appreciation is much more sophisticated and hopeful than that of our childhood because we have experienced much of what life has to offer and now choose to attribute meaning to the simple things with a deeper perception of their enormous value.

Think about the simple pleasures you've enjoyed in the past or are enjoying right now; become aware of their significance in your life. I'm not talking about major events, but simple pleasures. Make a list of them—whether it's listening to the rain, enjoying a piece of chocolate, or smelling the ocean air—and refer to it when you are feeling low or depleted of energy.

In the introduction, I described a woman with terminal breast cancer who I visited daily to change her dressing. I described as I changed her dressing, she might speak of a bird that had visited her birdfeeder that morning, or discuss her concerns for her husband when she was gone. I always

Diane S. Schaupp, Ph.D.

remember feeling very close to God as I left her home. Had I not been present with her during these moments, I would have missed these powerful exchanges.

At the end of life, life becomes very elementary and simple things take on a greater significance—simple but profound. Do not miss these moments. Every moment becomes a gift, an experience in mindfulness.

Learning to be still and centered is an important way to practice simplicity, but find any way that works for you. Here are some suggestions:

✝ Become centered through reading, gardening, walking, taking a bath. For some, centering might involve communicating with a higher power or with that wise person inside who knows you best. Others may choose to visualize someone who loves them very much. Imagine that this presence is filled with great love for you and is there to help you in whatever way you need. Or, visualize the most beautiful sky you have ever seen. Feel it. Breathe deeply.

✝ Set aside time for centering each and every day.

✝ Try journaling. This helps many people center.

✝ Singing and chanting repetitive words are also ways to center and have been practiced in many cultures for hundreds of year.

✝ Musical instruments help us reach the primal place inside. Music is thought to take us back to the first sound of our mother's heart.

Learning From Life's Lessons (Turning Lemons Into Lemonade)

What do you have to do for yourself to have peace of mind?

Are there things that happened to you that you would like to forgive?

Are there things you did that you haven't forgiven yourself for?

If you could change one decision that you've made, what would it be?

Some people are more comfortable with loose ends than others. If you feel there are areas in your life where you want to make peace, go ahead. It is not about expecting anything in return. This process is about you, and for you. It is one of the paths you can take toward peace of mind.

Forgiveness means letting go. When we carry resentment toward ourselves or others, we block the opportunity for growth. The end of unfinished business is forgiving yourself or another, the means whereby you can experience peace. By no longer judging, you release the past and your fear of the future. Forgiving means that you have learned and are no longer held hostage to negative feelings. Until you forgive someone, you are in competition with that person and you are losing.

Tying up unfinished business can be accomplished by something as simple as changing your outlook. For instance, I was plagued over the years by my father's lack of interest in me. Recently, I came to terms with all he had not done in his life and recognized he had been projecting his lack of self-worth onto me. I am grateful that my life has taken a different path and I feel sad for my father. I recognize I have many of his genes. I also recognize how hard it must have been for him to have had so few opportunities to actualize himself. Even if a person is dead, you can write an unsent letter dealing as fully as you can with the issue. Letting go in this way allows you to finish unfinished business.

With acts that are unforgivable and that would violate our own integrity and leave us vulnerable to more abuse if we forgive them, there is still a path we can take: we can concentrate on forgiving the perpetrator for having temporarily lost his or her humanity.

However, the person whom we often find hardest to forgive is ourselves. To facilitate the process, acknowledge that there is no way to go through life without making mistakes on occasion. Being hard on ourselves depletes our energy and gets us nowhere. Self-forgiveness breaks the cycle. Try saying to yourself, "For my own integrity and survival, I choose to no longer give away any of my energy. I choose to be in charge of myself. I choose to let go of this and no longer give my energy away over it!"

Forgiveness is not something that can be rushed. In thinking about forgiveness, we need to be able to validate our feelings of anger first. Only then is it possible to determine that it is not worth our energy to hang on to hard feelings any longer.

Regardless of how the forgiveness occurs, it is worth it. The change that happens enables us to finally appreciate each moment and live life so fully that "being" takes the backseat to "doing."

Drawing Strength

We can't go through life all alone. Being with those with whom we feel safe and secure enough to open our inner selves to, empowers us to become a better person. It is what life is all about. To me, it is the heart of a life well lived.

We've all experienced being supported and told not to give up. Yes, you *can* do it. And you can get through anything when you have the support and love of those whom you trust and respect. However, as much as we use the safety of close friendships from which to draw encouragement, those same friendships also can be the place where we can get a hard dose of reality when we need it. Because we trust one another, we can open up, and in return we can hear the truth and value the feedback. This feedback can keep us focused on living the life we want to live.

What works for me is drawing strength and encouragement from the small group of friends with whom I have relationships—those whom I trust and whose truth I value. I can't stress enough the importance of being with people who have the same qualities and hold the same set of values. However, at the same time, it is important to recognize that putting faith in others rather than ourselves and what is in front of us is a mistake. If we keep looking for the next guru to help us change our life, we miss out on precious opportunities for growth. Believing in ourselves is the first step in taking advantage of the abundance within us.

When that does not do it, reach out to help someone else. Yes, that's right: someone else. When my mother-in-law was staying with us after being told she was dying, she had a chance to visit with a colleague of mine who had stopped by to talk about the struggles her young son was having with an autoimmune disorder. My mother-in-law was feeling down that day from thinking about her impending death. As she heard my friend's story, she recognized she was not alone. She was not the only one living with troubles; there was someone else who also was struggling—and that person struggling was much younger. When my mother-in-law reached out to my colleague, she forgot her own struggles for a time. It is invigorating to have these intimate exchanges with others.

So what is your inner life like? Take a moment and analyze where you are. When the going gets tough, do you tell yourself that you will do whatever it takes to make things happen? Or, do you complain and make excuses? Reminder, with a positive attitude, there is not much you can't accomplish. Telling yourself how good your life is right now and how things can only get better will make your life better. You will live a better life despite the inevitable changes that the autumn of life brings.

So go ahead. Change lemons into lemonade. Fulfill your unrealized potential.

Endnote

1. Gail Sheehy, "Life Begins at 60," Parade Magazine (December 11, 2005): 4–6.

Chapter 12
Fulfilling Unrealized Potential

What change do we experience when we take on new roles! The growth and changes we make at age 60 and after may mean reworking, making peace with, or putting an end to previous arrangements we've made in every area of our lives as we move further along in our life cycle. There's much that can be positive about the changes we make, including the fact that they help us regain or fulfill the potential we suppressed earlier in life because of societal expectations or roles that were important for us to master back then.

For instance, in retirement, a woman may decide to reduce her hours in her career and serve in more of a consulting role. Because her career history may have been reduced with child rearing, she may not be as ready as her husband to retire from work completely. At the same time, although she may feel she has more to contribute at work, she may want more time to spend with grandchildren and friends now. She may want to give a smaller part of her heart to her work and a larger part to her private concerns.

For a man who spent a lifetime in the business world, he may begin to accept the limitations of his pursuit of future achievements and decide it's time to foster the careers of younger people. Or he may retire from the business world fully in pursuit of activities that have always interested him, whether they be carpentry, physical fitness, traveling, or cooking.

For both sexes, this time period also can serve as an opportunity for renewing the vitality in their most intimate of relationships, although how this occurs can vastly differ from one marital relationship to the next: "From this new dynamic, many different forms of marriage may follow: two very separate lives in which husband and wife come together only periodically, as their rhythm of relating dictates; total sharing of one's life in work and leisure; or variations between the two extremes."[1]

Much of the psychological changes that we encounter at this stage of life go a long way toward allowing us to complete ourselves—if we are flexible and allow ourselves to accept our new reality and life's expansiveness.

Reclaiming Our Potential After Child Rearing

When we are born, we possess a tremendous capacity for new learning and a large reserve of unformed cognitive and social potentials. Vulnerable because of our physical and intellectual dependence on our caregivers, we need nurturing of each of our potentials (i.e., for mastery and for nurturance) in order to develop into a truly functioning human being.

Allowing a human infant the freedom to develop requires a certain constraint of his or her behaviors on the part of his or her parents. For instance, it is better for a child to have one steady caregiver, so one parent opts to be that caregiver.

Diane S. Schaupp, Ph.D.

The other parent may opt to be the provider even though he or she might prefer spending more time with the child. Psychologist David Guttman calls the parenthood period of human adulthood "the parental emergency" as parents sacrifice their own inner development for the practical necessities of raising children.[2]

Our engagement in today's child rearing practices continues to reinforce traditional gender roles and those certain human characteristics that are specifically assigned according to gender. For example, nurturance has been considered a feminine attribute while assertiveness has been considered a masculine attribute. Staying at home with the children, providing them with emotional security, and assuming many of the responsibilities for their daily care have been viewed as reflective of the woman's role, while the man's role traditionally has been that of the familial provider and protector. Engaging in these roles does not permit individuals to enjoy and amplify the full range of psychological possibilities that are potentially within them. Often the woman yearns for more stimulation outside the home, while the man would like more leisure time to pursue hobbies and time with the children.

Gender-role training begins early in life, but as young women and men we still are allowed to indulge in a wide range of behaviors that enable us to develop our psychological potentials. Women obtain advanced degrees and participate in sports, for example. After the onset of marriage and children, however, we can never completely relax into self-absorption or self-indulgence.

As dedicated parents, no longer can we both enjoy and amplify the full range of psychological possibilities within us. Children come first—at a personal cost. A man or woman may decide to delay a career move or promotion if he or she feels it may impact a child negatively; a parent of either sex may set aside a passionate pursuit of golf or skiing if it means extended periods away from his or her child.

Fortunately, during this time women and men can regain externally what they lost internally through mating with another. A wife or girlfriend who represses her assertive and mastering side can identify with those same characteristics exhibited by her husband or boyfriend; a man who curtails his nurturing and tender side can identify with those traits exhibited by his wife or mate.[3]

As the years pass, the parental emergency phases out and parents have less need to live within the altruistic mode. Having raised the next generation of viable and procreative children, they now can reclaim the parts of themselves that were repressed. They can afford the luxury of elaborating the potentials and pleasures that they had to relinquish early on in the service of their particular tasks. Just as men in later life reclaim title to their denied "femininity," later women repossess the aggressive "masculinity" that they once lived out through their husbands. Women can tolerate and even enjoy the aggressiveness that once might have alarmed their children and alienated their male providers. They take over some of the drive toward dominance that had been previously the province of the male. At the same time, men are freed to recapture the duality of their own nature. They become more tender and nurturing. Besides reclaiming some of the cast-off parts of their feminine psyche, men also reclaim the full spectrum of emotions that their now-grown children have, in turn, abandoned by becoming adults.

As we are liberated from the parental emergency and enter the "normal androgyny" of middle age and after,[4] aging men and women disengage from their life in society while working to improve life in society. Often they take on the

Diane S. Schaupp, Ph.D.

executive function of the extended family by continuing to parent their adult children and providing the spiritual wisdom, grace, and courage on which family life depends. Guttman writes: "These parents receive uniquely important support (beyond mere babysitting) from the older men and women of the communities.[5] In fact, according to Guttman, our children will not succeed at rearing their own children without our support: "The unbuffered [unsupported] nuclear family does appear to be increasingly incapable of raising children who can avoid addictions, who do not need cults or charismatic totalitarian leaders, who can grow up parental in their own right."[6] Aging women who reclaim their hidden aggression use it openly within senior parental roles and in social life. At the same time, aging men, through their humility, conserve culture and the idealized systems that preserve social order. For instance, they reinforce the importance of family values, which might include religion, ethics, family history, and political theology. In this way, they provide meaning and significance to social life.[7]

Guttman also hypothesizes that later adults have the potential to transform the brains of children by encouraging new learning and creativity. He argues that children not only need their biological parents but also their extended family during the long periods of childhood dependency. In encouraging the appetite for new learning, later adults thus serve as "wardens of our previous human heritage" who help ensure "the successful transformation of cortical possibilities into executive capabilities of the human ego."[8] Guttman concludes, "We do not have elders because we have a human gift…for keeping the species alive; we are human *because we have elders* [emphasis mine]."[9]

In Guttman's research,[10] he also found that as later adult men relinquish their psychological appetite for taking life (i.e., as in war), and as later adult women relinquish their appetite for giving life (i.e., as in childbirth), they reveal a previously hidden body/mind combination suited to stability and continuity. Leaving a legacy helps achieve this equilibrium/stability. Additionally, as later adults are faced with debilitating physical, social, and existential changes, they are reactively driven to seek out and identify themselves with the eternal—for example, through having grandchildren, leaving a legacy, and thinking of an afterlife.

Because of their personal history and life experience, later adults serve as pathfinders to those in the world who will ultimately enter the realm of aging. For example, all cultures amplify myths—stories that tell how the gods or "unordinary" individuals interweaved in some special way at some special juncture. Examples of unordinary, older individuals would be Moses who brought the children out of Israel and George Washington who achieved victory against great odds to become a Founding Father of our country. Guttman writes that later adults become living examples of legends as it is through later adult women and men that the mythic past and mundane present are integrated. Aging women and men are able to tell the stories, make the connections, and see the parallels and patterns through their knowledge, experiences, and wisdom.

Later adults traditionally also have served to bridge the divine realm with the mundane world, making the abstract spiritual world accessible to the community by translating the stories into everyday behaviors, as in the story of the boy who cried wolf. Later adults also served as counsel chiefs, settling tribal disputes and guiding adolescents through rites of passage that prepared youth to assume adult responsibilities and carry on cultural traditions. Finally, they helped escort the soul into the afterlife as a kind of death counselor.

Diane S. Schaupp, Ph.D.

When we look at historical records, it is clear that over time later adults and elders have demonstrated the strength and usefulness of the aged in society. Without these role models, the world would lack maps about the place and significance of age in the life cycle.

Reclaiming Our Unfulfilled Potentials in Mourning

The mourning process helps us adapt, grow, and redefine ourselves in order to understand and cope with loss. In fact, psychoanalysis George Pollack says, "Success [in mourning] is far more than making the best of a bad situation. Mourning can lead to creative change."[11]

We have read about Mary, who found what was right for her after the loss of her husband, and Margaret, who turned failures into triumphs, returning to college after the passing of her husband and is now helping migrant workers learn English. Painful as these women's losses were, what they lost cleared the way for new development.

In Necessary Losses,[12] Judith Viorst takes the reader through a series of losses beginning with our first separation and loss: that of our symbiotic connection to our mothers. She describes how we lose the "paradise of oneness" to become ourselves. Yet identification with others is how we continue to develop our sense of self. For example, identification is why I value sociability and connection like my mother. Identification is why I value nature like my father. Identification is why I pay attention to details like my husband.

The people we identify with, positive or negatively, are always important to us. We often identify with a person whom we lose, symbolically or otherwise, in order to deal with their loss. In this way, we preserve them within ourselves.

Identifications serve simultaneously as both a way to hang on and a way to let go. We are often unconsciously saying, "I don't need you to do it, I'll do it myself." For instance, Margaret thought her husband was very intelligent. When he passed, she recognized that she also was intelligent. Returning to college reinforced her intelligence. As long as her husband was alive she identified with his intelligence. When he passed, she took that aspect of the relationship into herself.

Once we have taken in the parts of a loved person through identification, we begin to let go and move on from their loss. We recognize we will have some representation of the person for as long as we live if we choose to, and we find comfort in this acknowledgement. For many, they become aware of other parts of themselves that remained dormant during the life of the relationship (like Margaret), whether this is because of the parental emergency or the lifestyle developed by the couple. Although a sense of loss continues to be felt for a long time through "anniversary and birthday reactions," a new sense of freedom develops.

Remember the excitement that occurs when a toddler is exploring the world separate from Mom? There is an occasional looking back, but the curiosity of the world and the newfound capabilities are profound for the toddler. So it is when a mourning person begins to let go and move on, reclaiming his or her unfulfilled potential.

How fortunate it is that we are trained throughout life to form new relationships and create new identities. This preparation is helpful to us in later life when there are so many losses.

Diane S. Schaupp, Ph.D.

Reclaiming Our Innocence and Spontaneity From Childhood

As we reflect on our formative years, we come to reclaim and harness some of the untamed feelings of our childhood. In so doing, we become more empathetic, more lusty, more daring, more honest, more creative.

With the ability to abandon social convention, aging adults are able to reclaim childhood spontaneity. They integrate innocence and sagacity, uniting a child's native creativity with mature judgment. Additionally, when they affirm life as it is with a long process of self-confrontation, they liberate their long-forgotten child. Understood and nurtured, their innocence blossoms when they reclaim the wonder and delight in life. The return of wonder resembles what many spiritual traditions refer to as "enlightenment."

Aging gives us freedom to ignore social convention, but there is a caveat: The innocence and spontaneity I am referring to here implies a coming to terms with our egocentricity which differs from childhood.

Psychologist Abraham Maslow,[13] through a systematic investigation, identified a second innocence in his subjects (who were ages 50 and over) who had realized their full personal potential. These women and men broke from cultural norms to pursue their own creative insights, emancipating themselves from convention and "rationality." They also transcended their own egocentric concerns by absorbing themselves in their work and pursuing projects irrespective of public reward. To them, personal recognition mattered less than the creative work itself. According to Maslow, these self-actualized individuals acted in a spontaneous, expressive way similar to the innocence exhibited by children.

Embracing Our Darker Side to Reclaim Our Creativity

Unifying the opposite tendencies in our nature is a note-worthy accomplishment for later adults. The process of unifying the opposite tendencies of our nature began in childhood, when we reconciled the split between good and bad and learned to balance our wish for connection with our wishes to be separate and free.

As aging adults, we embrace our darker side, with an end result of freeing our creativity. Analyst Elliot Jacques, studying the development of creative artists, writes that "the aging artist's work changes when he recognizes the existence of hate and destructive impulses inside." He goes on to say that our creative nature depends on our constructive resignation "to hate and death in the midst of life."[14]

Although embracing our "darker side" may seem to be something that we should shun, Judith Viorst astutely and accurately observes that in freeing ourselves to acknowledge our darker center, "We can let ourselves know how we feel without automatically acting upon these feelings: We will find that acknowledged feelings are easier to control than those that are denied."[15]

Indeed, according to Roger Gould, we need to "connect with the insane in us before we can go on to a larger sanity."[16] He also says that the discovery of our darker side frees our energy and passion and revitalizes our life.[17] The challenge is to learn to integrate them in new ways.

Diane S. Schaupp, Ph.D.

Facing Our Own Death

Sigmund Freud's theory of the quality of life and death and how it plays out in our life helps our aging selves come to terms with the opposing psychological forces of life and death. Our life (*libido*) force surges with vitality, seeking pleasure and continuity of experience. Our death (*thanatos*) force yearns to return to an inanimate state of quiescence devoid of all striving and conflict. Life longs for us to experience sexual gratification and creative activity; death drives us toward annihilation and the cessation of activity. As we all know, death wins out in the end.

We have found that when we repress our death force, we lose energy. When we acknowledge our fear of death, we reclaim energy that has gone into supporting this denial. Streams of creative energy move through our bodies, minds, and nervous systems. "When we confront our mortality, a shift occurs that makes us more aware of how precious life really is," says psychologist David Feinstein. "We have an enhanced ability to accept ourselves along with a greater ability to love. We lose the pervasive anxiety that makes us grasp obsessively for power, wealth, and fame. As we discover a deepened sense of purpose and a profound connectedness with other people, we tend to be motivated by higher, more universal values, such as love, beauty, truth, and justice."[18]

Despite the psychological benefits of facing our inevitable death, many continue to deny and distort their attitudes. As later adults, we must work against our culture's denial of death and welcome an acceptance of our death. The struggle between life (libido) and death (thanatos) is an ongoing dialogue between the personality and the inner self. An outgoing force, our libido is concerned with survival and the sheer quality of experience. It pushes us into the peripheral of life, where we increase our connections with the world by starting new projects and relationships. An ongoing force concerned with life completion and self-actualization, thanatos takes us away from the peripheral. We become more selective in our relationships and the projects that we undertake as we deepen our connection to our inner self.

As we grow older and thanatos begins to assert itself, the polarity shifts in our consciousness. As the force of thanatos impacts us, we begin to experience decreased energy and an awakening sense of our inner life. It is at these points that we honor our thanatos by becoming more self-reflective as our actions become more discriminating.

In referring to later adulthood, Carl Jung asserted, "Aging people should know that their lives are not mounting and expanding but that an inexorable inner process enforces the contraction of life. For a young person, it is almost sin, or at least danger, to be too preoccupied with himself; but to the aging person it is a duty and a necessity to devote serious attention to oneself."[19]

It seems from middle age on, thanatos helps us become more contemplative by setting limits on our libidinal activities. Quantity of life experience is replaced with quality of life experience. Our expanding ways of behavior are replaced by more contemplative, reflective ways of being. In youth, our libido is transmitted in preserving the genetic family. As we age, the same libido passion is focused on leaving a legacy through writing, teaching, and creating oral histories. We are passing on wisdom rather than passing on genetic endowments.

The thanatos/death instinct has the potential of bringing together the fruits of our labor. Thanatos acts in the psyche to arrange into patterns of meaning all that we have begun in our lifetime. The conflict that ensues in midlife, and again

Diane S. Schaupp, Ph.D.

at age 60, is the using up of thanatos from the unconscious and demanding a place in our libido-driven life. When we deny the presence of our thanatos force, we compromise ourselves greatly. Our choice leaves us leading a shallow life that would not be the case if we embraced our thanatos inner force.

An example of a person who is denying the death instinct—or as Zalman Schachter-Shalomi[20] calls the "Life Completion Instinct"—would be someone who is having cosmetic surgery. An example of a man who is embracing thanatos is one who would want to spend more quality time with family, taking walks, and sharing dreams. According to Germaine Greer, author of *The Change*, postmenopausal women experience "a feeling of tenderness so still and deep and warm that it gilds every grass blade and blesses every fly."[21] When we accept our mortality, each moment becomes more profound, more vivid. Throughout history, the special powers of these women have been associated with healing, compassion, and a holistic understanding of how to act in harmony with the cycles of nature. A post-menopausal woman who embraces thanatos might tell her family she loves them but would like to live out another role that is clamoring for expression.

If we listen to our inner self and embrace thanatos, we will come to our life's completion with a sense of inner peace and tranquility. If we fight thanatos, our mature self will experience intense pain as it rebels against thanatos and our dwindling physical energies.

Completing Ourselves as Life Takes on New Meaning

As we age, we continue the process of recognizing and integrating opposite forces within ourselves. As we know, some of these opposing forces were quieted to prepare us for child rearing, while others remained silent because of a lifestyle choice such as coupling. Other potentials were quieted so we could fit into a societal norm, or because we learned to behave a certain way to be loved or to protect ourselves from pain. Lastly, when we were younger, we were filled with the life instinct. With aging, we are facing our death or life completion instinct, which turns us inward and helps us begin to recognize patterns of meaning in our life.

In unifying seemingly opposite tendencies, we are able to recognize our feminine and masculine self and move toward androgyny. We come to reclaim and harness some of the untamed feelings of our childhood; we see how our inner and outer destructiveness interferes with our creative self; and we begin to acknowledge a self that must die with a self that thrives on connection and immortality. We continue to struggle with these opposing forces in the autumn of life. We can't turn back, even though there are days we would like to do so. Our thanatos, or life completion instinct, keeps pushing us forward.

Through acknowledging thanatos, we are learning how to complete ourselves. We are working on our life review with the expectation of rewriting our past and forgiving and reclaiming our unfulfilled potential. As we reshape our thoughts about ourselves, our life takes on a new meaning.

Embracing our quieter, more authentic voice, we experience gratitude for our participation in life and the contributions we were able to make. Accepting the inevitable way our life unfolded, we understand better the continuity of life.

Diane S. Schaupp, Ph.D.

Endnotes

1. Roger Gould, *Transformations* (New York: Simon & Schuster, 1978), p. 291.

2. David Guttman, *Reclaimed Powers* (New York: Basic Books, 1988), p. 196.

3. David Guttman, p. 194.

4. David Guttman, p. 233.

5. David Guttman, p. 231.

6. David Guttman, p. 232.

7. David Guttman, p. 253.

8. David Guttman, p. 253.

9. David Guttman, p. 228.

10. David Guttman, p. 229.

11. George Pollack, "The Mourning Process and Creative Organizational Change," *Journal of the American Psychoanalytic Association* 25 (1, 1977): 3-34.

12. Judith Viorst, *Necessary Losses* (New York: Ballantine Books, 1989), p. 47.

13. Abraham Maslow, *Motivation and Personality* (New York: Harper & Row, 1970).

14. Elliot Jacques, "The Midlife Crisis," in Stanley Greenspan and George Pollack, eds., *The Course of Life*, Vol. 3 (Washington, DC :Government Printing Office, DHHS Pub. No. [ADM] 81-1000, 1981), p. 296.

15. Judith Viorst, p. 315.

16. Roger Gould, p. 305.

17. Roger Gould, p. 295.

18. David Feinstein, *Rituals for Living and Dying* (New York: Harper Collins, 1990).

19. Carl Jung, *Memories, Dreams, Reflections* (New York: Vintage Books, 1965).

20. Zalman Schachter-Shalomi, *From Aging to Saging* (New York: Time Warner, 1995).

21. Germaine Greer, *The Change: Women, Aging and the Menopause* (New York: Alfred A. Knopf, 1992).

Diane S. Schaupp, Ph.D.

Chapter 13

The Continuity of Life

Aging successfully not only involves understanding our past through understanding our life story and the cycles of life; it also involves reorienting ourselves in time. When we become rooted in the vast, timeless universe, we begin to lose our short-sighted views and develop a perspective of the world that connects us to all living matter. This new perspective helps us appreciate how our actions will impact future generations and the future of the world. We are transmitters of tradition, guardians of ancestral values, and providers of continuity.

Over the centuries, many archetypes have inspired us to look inward to find our lost potential. The peaceful smiling face of Buddha represents all present and future forms. Buddha orients us against a background of transcendent meanings and purposes. When we think this way, our life becomes transformed into one of unshakable serenity with a vision of time as being that of a gift.

Finding Our Inner Buddha

In *Memories, Dreams, Reflections*, Carl Jung[1] found images in our unconscious that shape our behavior, values, and creative capabilities. These images are called archetypes. According to Jung, archetypes are inborn within us. They are part of our inheritance as members of the human race. We can recognize the influence of an archetype when we see that the events of life fall into general patterns that are shared by people worldwide, regardless of cultural or religious differences.

Archetypes have shaped our behavior over time. For example, the Goddess archetype, which represents woman's inner strength and wisdom, played a powerful role in empowering humankind during the women's movement and the ecology movement. The recovery movement took the archetype of the inner child to represent a sense of hope and renewal to which people who embarked on this path could aspire. Recently, the archetype of the inner elder, which represents the wisdom of the ages, has been stirring in our collective psyche as baby boomers defy the more negative images of aging. Buddha is an archetype that activates our developmental potential in later life, moving us toward a state of self-realization called "enlightenment."

When we are impacted by an inner elder archetype such as Buddha, we break free of personal ambitions and hold up an image based on self-knowledge, transcendence of the personal ego, and a willingness to serve society as a mentor and teacher of the young. According to psychiatrist Allan Chinen,[2] transcending the aging process in this way is deep and overwhelming, requiring the acquirement and exhibition of our wisdom and patience necessary for the role of mentor. Higher concerns now dominate personal desires. Often the

Diane S. Schaupp, Ph.D.

higher self, society, or God replaces the ego as the guiding force of our lives.

Besides balancing our culture's myopic view of heroism with wisdom, the archetype of the inner elder expands our notion of time. Living between the apex of time and eternity, aging adults ask, "What is the meaning of my life? What have I contributed to make a difference in the world?"

Historically, the Native American culture provides examples of aging adults who made decisions in light of their affect on several generations. For instance, aging Native Americans might have considered the impact of cutting wood for a home and the impact of removing the trees on soil erosion and subsequent farming. Making decisions in this way reflects a deepened sense of time and responsibility. We, too, can serve to instill hope in the future by the considerations we have for the generations that come after us.

Unfortunately, in our culture, we all too often see aging adults who hold onto what they have for personal survival. These aging adults resist change, hold on to power in a tight-fisted manner, and impose unsolicited knowledge onto others. In contrast, an evolving aging adult who represents the continuity of life is one who posses an inner authority. Such people radiate a beneficial influence by evoking the spirit of young people. Because these evolving aging adults are in touch with the stories of the past, they transmit an understanding that helps young people meet the challenges of the present and the future. Without the continuity of the past, young people stay too focused on the present and lose the significance of the past for new learning and a sense of continuity.

Still, a delicate balance must be achieved between appreciation of the past and bringing in new views. If new views are not brought in, tradition grows stagnant, which eventually destroys creativity and intellectual curiosity. As evolving aging adults, we recognize that to be effective in dealing with today's problems, traditions of the past must be *built upon*, not destroyed or preserved. Evolving aging adults do not impose solutions; they create a dialogue between the generations, which reminds them of the consequences of their actions while trusting in the ability of the younger generation to listen and then make wise decisions. In these ways, evolving aging adults have the potential of restoring our culture to psychological health and equilibrium.

The first challenge we face in the final third of life is dealing with physical decline and multiple losses. In the process, we must be willing to delve into the unconscious, grappling with psychological issues that were intolerable to face in our youth. Yet age and experience provide a new strength to face old fears, and the challenge of maturity is to use those assets to grow. Ultimately, our new openness to experience depends upon confronting the darker side of our human nature—emotions such as anger over the indignities of aging, despair over multiple losses, envy for what younger people still possess, and greed for more in life.

The second challenge is self-confrontation and self-reformation. From self-confrontation comes an understanding of evil that, in turn, gives rise to worldly wisdom. The third challenge is to turn from the youthful preoccupation with things to an empathetic understanding of human nature. In a sense, wisdom is a reward for this honest self-confrontation. Survival and adaptation are not the ultimate goals of life during this time, however. We soon confront a new and more difficult challenge: self-transcendence.

It is ironic that the focus of the first two-thirds of life is establishing the self, while in the final third of life, the challenge is to leave the hard-won self behind. Ideally, the mature

Diane S. Schaupp, Ph.D.

adult returns to the transcendent inspirations of his or her youth, but in a deeper way with greater understanding and with the means to actualize some of the dreams. Transcendent inspirations take precedence over purely personal desires.

The fourth challenge is to heed the dictates of the soul, purified through a long process of self-confrontation and self-transcendence. We can affirm our life just as it is with all its joys, sorrows, and disappointments. When our life is understood and nurtured, a new innocence evolves that renews our experience of the world. The world is no longer taken for granted, and each object becomes an occasion for delight. This return of wonder resembles enlightenment or peak moments.

The final task is not one of personal illumination, but using our illumination or enlightenment to help the next generation. The last of life becomes the first, uniting wisdom and innocence, pragmatism and magic. The end is the beginning, renewed and restored.

Cultivating the Continuity of Life in Everyday Life

In early adulthood, we had to narrow our world vision to build a separate identity and to pursue our private ambitions. By narrowing our world vision, we were able to succeed in the practical affairs of life. But, as evolving aging adults, we are able to take back a broader world view. Overcoming the split between world and self, timelessness and time, we attune ourselves with the larger source from which we initially separated and return to a state of wholeness.

When we, as evolving aging adults, activate the elder archetype of wisdom and timelessness, we bridge the spiritual and material worlds with acts of everyday kindness that benefit individuals and the world community.

We also can cultivate the continuity of life by taking long walks in nature, as often this connects us with deeper, more meditative aspects of consciousness. For example, recently I was walking on the beach in Costa Rica with my daughter-in-law. We stopped to watch the labor of a minute sand crab carrying its shell. We watched the small creature unload its tiny shell. Then it pushed its body into a larger shell and proceeded to pull itself forward into its new life. We commented on how vulnerable the crab is until they find another shell. "It has to work so hard to shed its smaller shell for a larger shell. So, it is with change." We both looked at each other with amazement!

Cultivating a garden helps deepen our awareness of time by acquainting ourselves with nature's slow, unhurried rhythms. Going out each morning before work, I marvel at the surprises which are awaiting me—such as the dramatic blooming of a flower—from the insignificant, almost imperceptible changes that take great stretches of time to unfold. Creative activities such as music, dance, painting, and poetry also evoke the evolving aging adult.

We also can practice a technique called "active imagination"—developed by Carl Jung—in which we hold dialogue with images from our unconscious. This technique involves posing a question to our inner wise old woman or wise old man, and entering into a dialogue. The dialogue here is not directed, but flows quietly from the unconscious. This form of imagination is active, says Jungian analyst Richard Johnson,[3] because we consciously go into the inner world and engage figures in conversation, exchange points of view, and learn by listening to the unconscious. By giving the unconscious an equal voice, we can consciously work on issues without waiting for clarification from dreams.

Another way to cultivate the continuity of life is through rites of passage. Throughout history, women and men have undergone ritualized public ceremonies to help their transition from one stage of life to another. These ceremonies enable us to leave an outworn stage of life behind and to invest ourselves with a new identity, new roles, and a new way of being in the world.

For aging adults, rites of passage formally sever our ties from midlife goals, replacing them with the wider concerns of elderhood. For example, in a ceremony attended by family and friends, Japanese people celebrate their 60th birthday by donning red garments that announce their new status. The clothing indicates liberation from social obligations and a return to the innocence and freedom of childhood. In the Native American community, postmenopausal women are initiated into the Grandmother Lodge, which is comprised of a tribal support group of women who wish to explore and develop wisdom. Meeting on a regular basis, these women turn their attention to the inner, contemplative life that was sacrificed on the altar of parental necessity. For women in the Grandmother Lodges, this pledge to nurture the world might take the form of volunteering in schools, helping immigrants learn English as a second language, espousing environmental concerns, deepening spiritual contact through studying Shamanism, or dedicating themselves to teaching their grandchildren on an individual basis.

Jean Bolen, Jungian analyst and author of *Goddesses in Everywoman*,[4] has devised a powerful ritual to help postmenopausal women reclaim their wise woman archetype. The women gather on a private ranch in Montana where they develop bonds of friendship and trust by sharing stories about their lives. After the women have laughed and cried together, delighted in their triumphs and mourned their losses, Bolen leads them into an underground ritual cave where they seek rebirth through the wisdom that comes from the "nourishing dark." Sitting in a sacred circle, the women light a candle to illuminate the darkness. Then, one by one, they hold up the candle and speak about the wisdom they have learned in surviving. In this way, each participant claims the wise woman as her own.

According to Bolen, it is necessary for women to consciously revise the wise woman archetype because of the assaults on it and its devaluation over the centuries. The crone, or wise woman, initially commanded respect as a priestess, leader, midwife, and teacher. But during the Middle Ages, the Inquisition launched a campaign to suppress women's direct spiritual knowledge. Declaring wise women to be witches, the church persecuted them for a period of 300 years by portraying older women as ugly, foul, wrinkled, and useless to society.

Memories of these persecutions live on in the collective psyche of modern women, but when connected to the life-affirming image of the crone, women declare war on the misogynist stereotypes that keep them powerless. The crone invests a woman with a sense of inner wholeness and power, freeing her from the expectations of others and giving her an ability to act decisively in the world based on a commitment to higher values. "Many of today's post-menopausal women, who were active in the women's movement during the past three decades, are defining for themselves what a wise woman is and does in the 1990's," Bolen says. "Besides being autonomous and creative, the new wise woman has the courage and conviction to speak up in defense of the planet, the world's children, and the downtrodden in society, including men, oppressed races and elders. The return of the

Diane S. Schaupp, Ph.D.

wise woman archetype might help infuse our institutions with more compassion, so that we treat people humanely while operating in the long-term interest of the Earth and the next generation of children."[5]

Men's ceremonies, like women's rituals, have some of the same elements that help them leave behind their former identities while investing them with the responsibilities of elderhood.

Poet and men's movement guru Robert Bly gathers together men of all ages to tell their stories to the beating of drums. Other men go on weekend retreats with their religious communities. Still others might undertake a modified vision quest, spending quiet, contemplative time in nature reviewing their lives and seeking a vision of their new path.

Now that you understand how rites of passage into a new life stage works, you might want to participate in one or orchestrate one for someone you know. Whether you hold it outdoors or in a meeting room, whether you invite members of a larger community or a small group of friends, you can develop the event to fit your own requirements.

Each one of us has the capability to create beautiful ceremonies to help ourselves or our elders feel special, loved, and valuable. A rite of passage might involve something as simple as organizing a dinner in the park to honor an elder for his or her contribution to the community. It's a common tradition when someone retires that we launch that person into their new stage of life through a ceremony in which people express their appreciation through little speeches, poems, songs, dance, and artwork. But we also can create personalized rituals to commemorate our retirement, relocation, change in health status, menopause, or upcoming death. These help us to grow, allowing us to move through transitions in healthy and meaningful ways rather than in dysfunctional fashions. By cultivating the archetypal evolving aging adult or elder during such times, it encourages us to continue our journey into the unknown as we reach toward the state of fulfillment symbolized by our complete self. Awakening to the vast continuum of time, we provide the present with wisdom that the world so desperately needs.

Conscious Death and Spiritual Growth

The hospice movement began an important movement toward conscious dying. In *conscious dying*, actual death is viewed as the culminating movement of a lifetime that serves as a transition to other states of consciousness. Death is viewed not as a mortal enemy but as a birthright into continued growth. The death awareness movement even teaches death preparation techniques that make the transition as serene and fearless as possible.

Society today has demystified the transcendent nature of dying and reduced it to a pathological physical process managed by doctors. In accepting this, we have surrendered control over our own death. Yet many of us would rather die this way because our unavoidable appointment with mortality calls forth an anxiety that paralyzes us emotionally so that we cannot enter the experience with awareness.

Anya Foos-Graber, in her book, *Deathing*, [6] teaches techniques that allow us to leave the world consciously. These techniques are similar to those used for consciously birthing people into the world. Her methods include relaxation, breathing techniques, and mental focusing exercises that keep the person as undistracted as possible. This allows a person to encounter the light of expanded awareness with a serene, focused mind. Foos-Graber recommends having a trusted support person available to guide and coach the

Diane S. Schaupp, Ph.D.

dying person.

Tibetan Buddhists claim that because death represents the culmination of the life cycle and its most intense concentration of energy, whatever thoughts and feelings we hold accompany us and, to a large extent, determine the quality of our after-death experience. Buddhists therefore train the dying to attain a clear, meditative state of awareness devoid of fear and distraction. This clarity enables us to recognize the enlightened state of mind that appears at death, merge with it, and attain spiritual liberation.

There are many beliefs about the afterlife that allow us to experience spiritual growth. We could say that traditional Western religions—Christianity, Judaism and Islam—believe the human soul is independent of the physical body and continues in another form after death. What, then, dies when we die? According to Rabbi Zalman Schachter-Shalami, it appears that "we slough off only the physical part of our being. Once we are in touch with the entirety of our organism, we find it less threatening and fearful to handle the absence of the physical component. Realizing that we are rooted in a multi-dimensional universe, we sense that our departed loved ones do not just disappear into some kind of cosmic black hole, but continue in a different form. We also sense that we are connected with them even though we are physically separated."[7]

According to *The Tibetan Book of the Dead*, the deceased are particularly receptive to the heartfelt thoughts, feelings, and prayers on their behalf. We might say, "Dear friend, I send you loving supportive thoughts for the journey ahead. Do not be afraid; it's a shock to drop the body, but it's not the end of your existence. Now that you've abandoned your old, worn-out body, go forward to your new life in anticipation of a pain-free, comfortable existence. Go in trust and peace, knowing that friends and guides will appear to help you through this transition."[8]

Whether we believe in being recycled as a part of an ongoing existence or subscribe to life after death as taught by the world's spiritual traditions, or whether we synthesize the two views, as evolving aging adults we must finish our business in this world and begin to prepare for what occurs at life's exit. By confronting death in life, we come out of hiding and open our hearts to the human community. At the same time, we put aside our proud but pathological sense of separateness. Interdependent with the greater web of life, we no longer postpone our engagement with life. By confronting our own death, we in fact learn the art of living.

The Continuity of Life Through Mentoring

Mentoring is the art of intergenerational bestowal by which elders pass on the living torch of their wisdom to younger people. Mentors do not impose their values, but rather evoke the individuality of their mentees. They encourage them in their struggles to clarify their values and discover their authentic life paths. Mentors do not give answers, but help by deepening their ability to question and to search for meanings. If we are nonjudgmental with our mentees, they can talk about their failures and their indiscretions and foibles. But, what empowers a mentor to act in such compassionate ways?

The mentoring capability evolves in us when we have accumulated the wisdom of a lifetime and we begin to feel a strong passion inside of us to leave a legacy. This life force takes the form of mentoring and transmits our essence in a nonbiological way. Mentoring preserves valuable life experiences from disappearing with the inevitable decay of our

Diane S. Schaupp, Ph.D.

physical bodies.

Mentoring is a give-and-take relationship. As evolving aging adults, we have the life experience and wisdom. At the same time, the mentee, having more youthful energy, rejuvenates the mentor and provides a plethora of fresh ideas. Without this exchange, the mentor can remain locked in the past. With their forward-looking mentality, mentees give mentors the gift of encountering the present and anticipating the future.

When we become mentors, we teach more than technical information about our area of expertise: We impart lessons about living that become transferred to our mentee's personal circumstance.

Integrating Spirituality Into Our Human Development

In the new paradigm of aging, with its emphasis on lifetime learning, brain–mind development, and service to humanity, we are set in motion to develop our spirituality as part of human development. In considering development from this perspective, it is helpful to consider the four *ashramas* in Hindu society, which can provide a psychospiritual guide of the human life cycle.

According to this model, people have an important task in old age: self-realization and service to society. The four stages, or *ashramas*, each span 25 years, and serve as necessary stations in the soul's unfolding.

In this system of life span development, people pass through the student and householder stages to enter the forest-dweller stage at around age 50. Here they begin devoting greater amounts of time to spiritual development. Forest dwellers still fulfill social obligations, but they begin to withdraw in stages from their work and family identities as they cultivate the awareness, through meditation, that the world is their family. In the final stage, *sannyasa* or renunciation (which corresponds to retirement age in the West), they devote all their time and energy to self-realization. As citizens of the world who have moved beyond the pursuit of wealth, position, and power, they increasingly identify with the inner self. Detached and emotionally unruffled by life's contingencies, they serve society by imparting wisdom to those in the other three *ashramas*.

This traditional model has much to teach us. First, it helps us conceive of life as a spiritual journey with certain identifiable stages that lead naturally to a spiritual unfolding. Second, it implies that the latter years offer the greatest opportunity for self-realization. Seen from this perspective, all of life is a preparation for old age and its crowning task of self-development. Third, it encourages us to begin to cultivate a spiritual life in middle age, so that when retirement detaches us from productive work, we don't fall into socially induced uselessness. We have a full-time vocation that gives our lives meaning: developing wisdom and making it available for the well-being of society.

Endnotes

1. Carl Jung, *Memories, Dreams, Reflections* (New York: Vintage Books, 1965).

2. Allan Chinen, *In the Ever After* (Wilmette, IL: Chiron Publications, 1989), pp. 139–148.

3. Robert Johnson, *Inner Work: Using Dreams and Active Imagination for Personal Growth* (New York: Harper & Row, 1986).

4. Jean Bolen, *Goddesses in Everywoman: A New Psychology of Women*. (New York: Harper & Row, 1984).

5. Jean Bolen, p. 24.

6. Anya Foos-Graber, *Deathing: An Intelligent Alternative for the Final Moments of Life* (New Beach, ME: Nicolas-Hays, 1989).

7. Zalman Schachter-Shalomi, *From Aging to Saging* (New York: Warner Books, 1995), p. 141.

8. Sogyal Rinpoche, *The Tibetan Book of Living and Dying* (New York: Harper Collins, 1993), p. 20.

Chapter 14

Each Day, a Day to Enjoy

At 60, we are acutely aware that our time here is precious. We want to savor each moment. In so doing, we flourish rather than merely survive. But, we need to make time each day for how we really want to live our life if we are to flourish.

Below are some ideas that might help you focus more time on your inner journey. As you have learned through reading this book, the more you announce to yourself "I like this. This is really living!" The more you'll feel you are flourishing rather than just surviving in your life.

More About Affirmations

While it is important to insert affirmative thoughts into our minds if they are not already there, it is also important that they are believable. Before getting out of bed in the morning, get into the habit of focusing on something positive and good in your life. A patient of mine who struggled with anxiety and depression heard a psychiatrist on a news program advocating the importance of writing down three things to be grateful for each morning. This patient was very disciplined, and followed his advice. To her amazement, she felt better within two weeks.

Here are some suggestions for daily affirmations:

+ I have choices.

+ I am changing and that is good.

+ I am having a fulfilling and fun time as I age.

+ I will get through this.

+ I can make someone else feel good today.

+ I can choose where to direct my energy.

+ I accept myself unconditionally right now.

Humor

In his early 50s, the noted critic and *Saturday Review* editor Norman Cousins was stricken with a crippling form of arthritis. Shortly after he learned of his diagnosis, he fell into a deep depression. Doctors told him he needed some cheering up, so he called his friend Alan Funt, a producer of the *Candid Camera* TV show. Alan Funt shipped copies of several episodes of *Candid Camera*.

Cousins had a film projector set up in his hospital room; a nurse ran the episodes for him on it. In his bestselling *Anatomy of an Illness*,[1] Cousins recalled how much he laughed upon viewing the shows. He then cited scientific evidence suggesting that a deep hearty laugh can improve lung respiration, oxygenate the blood, and promote the body's production of *endorphins*, natural pain killers that enhance our general sense of well-being.

Diane S. Schaupp, Ph.D.

Each of us is well served by cultivating our individual funny bones: talking about cartoons that make us smile, telling jokes or anecdotes that paint life's ironies, going to movies that make us laugh, or watching TV shows that strike us as amusing. Once we have a better understanding and appreciation of our own sense of humor, it's much easier to make use of it when we really need it.

So what makes *you* laugh? Start a journal and write down what gives you a chuckle. It will prove handy when you need to be cheered up. Use the following questions as a springboard to start your humor journal:

✛ Who is the funniest person you know? Say something about her or him.

✛ Who do you know who has the best laugh?

✛ Name three things you enjoy doing with a child.

✛ When was the last time you had a good laugh? What about?

✛ Is your sense of humor more active with certain people? Who?

I put the following humorous vignette—given to me by a friend—into my humor journal:

Have you been guilty of looking at others your own age and thinking, surely I cannot look that old? While waiting for my first appointment in the reception room of a new dentist, I noticed his certificate, which bore his full name. Suddenly, I remembered that a tall, handsome boy with the same name had been in my high school class some 30 years ago. Upon seeing him, however, I quickly discarded any such thought. This balding, gray-haired man with the deeply-lined face was way too old to have been my classmate. After he had examined my teeth, I asked him if he had attended the local high school.

"Yes," he replied.

"When did you graduate?" I asked.

He answered, "In 1971. Why?"

"You were in my class!" I exclaimed.

He looked at me closely, and then the son-of-a-bitch asked, "What did you teach?"

A Positive Mood

Keeping a positive mood is necessary if we are to flourish rather than accept mere survival in later life. Reframing our self-talk is one way we keep our mood positive. As a reminder, *reframing* is the process of using more life-enhancing and hopeful words and concepts.

Personal Growth in Our Later Years

Some of the time you have set aside each day can be used to work on personal growth exercises. Some of you may choose to devote an hour each day to the task, while others may work for half an hour to 45 minutes a few times a week. The important factor is that your mood is good so you can receive a positive benefit from this time.

The time you allot to your personal growth is a gift to yourself. At the same time, it will not always leave you feeling happy and satisfied. At times, you will uncover territory that arouses your anxiety, so having the commitment and discipline to continue is important.

When you finish your personal growth exercises, reward yourself with something you enjoy. Hopefully, over time, this work will lead you to feel more open-hearted and available to the opportunities within yourself to heal the past and move on to reclaiming your unfulfilled potential. You also will discover that you are serving as a provider of continuity, a transmitter of tradition, and a guardian of ancestral values.

Journaling

Journaling can be an important tool for healing as well as a way to tell your story. If you choose to take time to reflect on your life through journaling, there are a number of benefits:

1. By writing your life story, you'll be able to take meaning from your life's journey.

2. Journaling provides an opportunity for personal integration. This means acknowledging all of life's experiences, good and bad, and fitting them together in a dynamic balance. By reliving the events and ups and downs of our life, we begin to integrate our separate parts.

3. Your personal history is an important part of your identity. Our past gives continuity and meaning to the present. We are much more than who we are in this moment.

4. Journaling provides a form of legacy. It is an opportunity to share who we are. Documenting our highs and lows, our memories of special and meaningful events and what we have learned, is a gift to leave those who follow. Our recorded journey can become their pathway. Our recorded journey is a vehicle for transmitting our values, our essence, and our hard-earned wisdom to other

generations. Something of us will live on. We are the link between the past and the future.

5. Through the self-reflection of journaling, we might be able to determine what we want to change to improve the quality of our life.

6. Our life story may uncover some deeply buried, hurtful memories, but the sharing of our hurtful memories often helps others better understand us and our behavior. Bringing other people into awareness is also helpful as it helps us remove blockages that prevent us from getting on with life and living more fully. Later adulthood is a time when truthfulness becomes more important. Self-acceptance evolves. We stop thinking things will be different than they are.

7. Through journaling, we learn to accept the mistakes we've made in the past and let go of them, to begin today anew. "This is how I want to live my life" is a great way to start the day. Leaving behind regrets and unproductive patterns helps us do this. Recalling mistakes and hard-learned lessons can be as important gifts to share in our journals as our successes.

8. Journaling helps us find out more than facts and memories. It is a "head-and-heart" exercise. By going back to our formative beginnings and matters of the heart through journaling, we get closer to the truth and source of meaning.

If you are having difficulty getting started with journaling, I recommend you read *Journal to the Self* by Kathleen Adams.[2]

Diane S. Schaupp, Ph.D.

Meditation

Don't try too hard to make things happen and don't try to stop things from happening. Just allow things to happen all by themselves, the way they need to unfold.

No matter what type of meditation you use, the important end product is mental gratitude. Meditation serves to quiet the mind. It has the capability to promote healing by impacting the autonomic nervous system (decrease heart rate, breath rate, muscle tension) and influence behavior, attitude, cognitive perceptions, and emotions.

> Don't try too hard to make things happen and don't try to stop things from happening. Just allow things to happen all by themselves, the way they need to unfold.

Meditation can also be used for unconscious exploration. It can help us get in touch with underlying dynamics, motivations, or unresolved feelings about past experiences that may be influencing you. Regular practice can help break the bad habit of ruminating over hurtful memories of the past. Meditation circulates streams of forgiveness, compassion, and intuitive insight throughout our body systems. Like a rudder, meditation also helps keep us on course as we move through life. As we develop contemplative skills and a grateful mentality, we keep to the middle path as we work patiently on the ongoing work of self-actualization.

Meditation helps us take control of our consciousness. As we practice meditation, we begin to notice that our attention improves. We experience more of the characteristics of personal adaptability and we feel cared for as we take this time for ourselves.

Many of these contemplative techniques have been tested in laboratory experiments. In *Quantum Healing*, Dr. Deepak Chopra,[3] an endocrinologist who advocates holistic approaches to medicine, reports on an experiment performed in 1980 by Harvard psychologist Charles Alexander. Alexander taught mind–body techniques to 80-year-old residents of three nursing homes in Boston. The residents practiced either relaxation techniques, Transcendental Meditation, or a set of word games to sharpen mental skills. Follow-up tests showed that the meditators scored the highest when improved learning abilities, low blood pressure, and mental health were measured.

Even more interestingly, when Alexander returned to the same nursing homes 3 years later, he found, to his surprise, that while one-third of the residents had died, the death rate was zero among the meditators. (*Meditators* were defined as residents who continued to meditate on a regular basis.) In understanding this finding, Chopra hypothesized that cellular activity is enhanced, which slows the aging process through meditation.

It thus seems that meditation does have many benefits in helping us claim a good quality of life by improving our level of consciousness.

There is no "generic" form of meditation, but you are probably familiar with meditative forms from the various religions of the world. To a Hindu, meditation might refer to mantra chanting. To a Christian, it might involve chanting prayers from memory or from a prayer book. For Jews, it might involve entering into the stillness pointed to by the Torah. To a Buddhist, meditation might refer to breath control and the observation of thoughts. To others, it might mean quieting the mind and receiving guidance from our unconscious mind and/or higher power.

Diane S. Schaupp, Ph.D.

Rituals

Throughout history, women and men have undergone ritualized pubic ceremonies to help them make the transition from one stage of life to another. These ceremonies enable us to leave a worn stage of life behind and invest ourselves with a new identity, new roles, and a new way of being in the world.

Ritualizing life passages publicly reinforces our commitment to grow in new ways. At the same time, we gracefully close the gates to the past and open new horizons for the future.

Our culture provides few rituals to help us adjust to transitions common in later life. Creating personalized ceremonies to commemorate menopause, retirement, relocation, change in health status, and death can help us move through these transitions.

Ceremonies that help us successfully move to 60 and after are important because up until recently the emphasis has been on the hero's journey. No matter how passionately we pursue the hero's journey, however, it ultimately takes us to our aging self, where we must surrender our role in society and continue into the uncharted territory we as aging adults are pioneering in the postindustrial, 21st century. By evoking wise archetypes during this transition, we receive encouragement to continue our journey into the unknown as we reach toward the state of fulfillment symbolized by our completed self.

Are You Ready to Start?

These are by no means the only techniques available to embrace your aging self. Be eclectic in assembling the tools that you need, pulling them from psychotherapists, spiritual guides, books, tapes, and even radio and television talk shows. What is important is your readiness to accept with enthusiasm your aging self so that you, too, will flourish.

Endnotes

1. Norman Cousins, *Anatomy of An Illness* (New York: W. W. Norton, 1979).

2. Kathleen Adams, *Journal to the Self* (New York: Time Warner, 1990).

3. Deepak Chopra, *Quantum Healing: Exploring the Frontiers of Mind/Body Medicine* (New York: Bantam Books, 1989).

Epilogue

The time had come for me to look courageously at my own aging self as so many of my family members and patients had done before me. In renewing my own life story, I've had to face my imperfect childhood, my imperfect mothering, my imperfect partnering, my imperfect friendships, my imperfect professional life!!! My own imperfect past had to be reencountered and acknowledged so I could embrace and accept myself fully. How could I write a book about psychological aging if I were not a fellow traveler with you on life's journey?

In my journey, I've discovered that to take risks, to meet challenges, and live life fully, there are joys, pain, and loss. I've learned that it is important to acknowledge and understand both the gains and losses of my previously encountered experiences. In so doing, the meaning in them can be translated to realistic, positive attitudes. This process involves tying up loose ends, completing unfinished business, forgiving, and letting go. I've learned too that there is great freedom in changing what can be changed and in achieving a sense of serenity by accepting what cannot.

It has been helpful to understand the psychological struggle I've encountered at the various stages of my life. I was able to identify my strengths and vulnerabilities. For instance, I recognize that although my patience and loyalty are strengths, they have also impacted my ability to make necessary life changes. I am thus mindful of sorting out my ambivalent feelings about making changes to move forward.

I am also aware that to craft a "new life" in the years ahead, I have to commit the same energy I committed to figuring out career path choices. I've found new meaning to the terms *self acceptance, personal adaptability,* and *interdependence.* My hope is that I've been able to communicate new meanings to you the reader of PRIME TIME.

I know all of what I have said may not make sense to you. But I hope what I have introduced in this book will challenge you and will help you embark on a journey to craft a "new life" for yourself.

Enjoy your journey!

Bibliography

Adams, Kathleen. Journal to the Self. New York: W.W. Norton, 1979.

Baltic, P.B. and J. Smith. "Toward a Psychology of Wisdom and Its Ontagenesis." in Wisdom: Its Nature, Origins and Development, edited by R. Steinberg, 87-120. New York: Cambridge Press, 1990.

Baum, Frank L. The Wizard of Oz. New York: Henry Halt, 1942.

Beers, Mark H., Thomas Jones, Michael Berkwits, Justin L. Kaplan, and Robert Porter. The Merck Manual of Health and Aging. Whitehouse Station, N.J.: Merck Research Laboratories, 2004.

Berry, Thomas. The Dream of Earth. San Francisco: Sierra Books, 1988.

Bolen, Jean. Goddess in Everywoman: A New Psychology of Women. New York: Harper and Row, 1984.

Brooks, Robert and Sam Goldstein. The Power of Resilience. New York: McGraw Hill, 2003.

Butler, Robert. "The Life Review: An Interpretation of Reminiscence in the Aged." in <u>Philosophical Foundations of Gerontology</u>, edited by Patrick L. McKee, 238. New York: Human Science Press, 1982.

Butler, Robert and Herbert P. Gleason, eds. <u>Productive Aging</u>. New York: Springer-Verlag, 1985.

Caine, Lynn. <u>Widow</u>. New York: Harper & Row, 1974.

Caplin, G. "Mastery of Stress: Psychological Aspects," <u>American Journal of Psychiatry</u>. 138: 413-420.

Chinen, Alan. <u>In the Ever After</u>. Wilamette, IL: Chinen Publications, 1989.

Chopra, Deepak. <u>Quantum Healing: Exploring the Frontiers of Mind/Body Medicine</u>. New York: Bantam Books, 1989.

Cole, Thomas. <u>The Journey of Life: A Cultural History of Aging in America</u>. New York: Cambridge Press, 1992.

Cousins, Norman. <u>Anatomy of an Illness as Perceived by the Patient</u>. New York: Bantam Books, 1981.

Covey, Stephan. <u>The Seven Habits of Highly Effective People</u>. New York: Simon & Schuster, 1989.

Csikszentmihalyi, Mihaly. <u>Creativity: Flow and the Psychology of Discovery and Invention</u>. New York: Harper & Collins, 1996.

deBeauvoir, Simone. <u>The Coming of Age</u>. New York: G. P. Putman, 1972.

DiGuilio, Robert C. Beyond <u>Widowhood: From Bereavement to Emergence and Hope</u>. New York: Free Press/MacMillan, 1989.

Dittman, Melissa. "A New Face to Retirement," <u>Monitor on Psychology</u>, 35, November, 2004.

Dychtwald, Ken and Joe Flower. <u>Age Wave</u>. New York: Bantam Books, 1990.

Edelson, Gerald. <u>Neural Darwinism</u>. New York: Basic Books, 1987.

Eissler, K. R. <u>The Psychiatrist and the Dying Patient</u>. New York: International Press, 1955.

Erikson, Erik. <u>Childhood and Society</u>. New York: Norton, 1950.

Flinstein, David. <u>Rituals for Living and Dying</u>. New York: Harper Collins, 1990.

Fischer, M. F. K. <u>Sister Age</u>. New York: Alfred A. Knopf, 1983.

Foos-Gerber, Anya. <u>Deathing: An Intelligent Alternative for the Final Moments of Life</u>. New Beach, ME: Nicolas-Hays, 1989.

Fredrickson, Barbara T. and Marical F. Losada. "Positive Affect and the Complex Dynamics of Human Flourishing," <u>American Psychologist</u>, 60, 678-684, 2005.

Franklin, Deborah. "The Healthiest Women in the World," <u>Health</u>, 57-64, September, 1996.

Friedan, Betty. <u>The Fountain of Age</u>. New York: Simon & Schuster, 1993.

Gerber, Jerry, Janet Wolff, Walter Klores, and Gene Braun. <u>Lifetrends: The Future Baby Boomers and Other Aging Americans</u>. New York: MacMillan, 1989.

Gilligan, Carol. <u>In a Different Voice</u>. Cambridge, MA: Harvard Press, 1982.

Glas, Norbert. <u>Fulfillment of Old Age</u>. New York: Steiner Books, 1987.

Goldman, Connie and Richard Mabler. <u>Secrets of Becoming a Late Bloomer</u>. New Hampshire: Stillpoint Publishing, 1995.

Goodheart, Annette. "Laugh Your Way to Health," <u>Science of the Mind</u>, 15, September, 1988.

Gores, Geoffrey. <u>Death, Grief and Mourning</u>. New York: Doubleday, 1965.

Gould, Roger. <u>Transformations</u>. New York: Simon & Schuster, 1978.

Green, Andrea. "Finals," The Sweet Annie and Sweet Pea Review. 11, 16-18, January, 2006.

Greer, Germaine. <u>The Change: Women, Aging, and the Menopause</u>. New York: Alfred A. Knopf, 1992.

Guttman, David. <u>Reclaiming Powers</u>. New York: Basic Books, 1988.

Hachschild, Arlie Russell. <u>The Unexpected Community: Portrait of an Old Age Subculture</u>. Berkeley: University of California, 1978.

Hayflick, Leonard. <u>How and Why We Age</u>. New York: Ballantine Books, 1996.

Hildebrand, Peter. <u>Beyond Midlife Crisis</u>. London: Sheldon Press, 1995.

Hollowell, Edward M. <u>Connect: 12 Vital Lies that Open Your Heart</u>. New York: Pantheon, 1999.

Jacques, Elliot. "The Midlife Crisis," in <u>The Course of Life</u>, 3, edited by George Pollack Washington, D.C.: Government Printing Office, DHHS Pub. No. CADM, 296, 1981.

Johnson, Robert. <u>Inner Work: Using Dreams and Active Imagination for Personal Growth</u>. New York: Harper & Row, 1986.

Jung, Carl. "The Stages of Life," in <u>The Portable Jung</u>, edited by J. Campbell. New York: Viking, 1974.

Jung, Carl. <u>Memories, Dreams, Reflections</u>. New York: Vintage Books, 1965.

Kegan, Robert. The Evolving Self: Problems and Process in Human Development. Cambridge, MA: Harvard University Press, 1982.

Keyes, C.L.M. "The Mental Health Continuum: From Languishing to Flourishing in Life." <u>Journal of Health and Social Behavior</u>, 43, 207-222, 2002.

Kidd, Sue Monk. <u>When the Heart Waits</u>. San Francisco, CA: Harper & Collins, 1992.

Kobasa, S. and M. Puccetti. "Personality and Social Resources in Stress Resistance." <u>Journal of Personality and Social Psychology</u>, 45, 4, 1983.

Kubler-Ross, Elizabeth. <u>On Death and Dying</u>. London: Collins-MacMillan, 1969.

Kushner, Harold. <u>When Bad Things Happen to Good People</u>. New York: Schacken Books, 1981.

Langer, Ellen and Judith Rodin. "The Effects of Choice and Enhanced Personal Responsibility for the Aged: A Field Experiment in an Institutional Setting." <u>Journal of Personality and Social Psychology</u>, 35, 897-912, 1977.

Lear, Martha. <u>Heart Sounds</u>. New York: Pocket Books, 1980.

Levy, Becca R. "Mind Matters: Cognitive and Physical Effects of Aging Stereotypes." <u>The Journals of Gerontology Sciences and Social Success</u>, 58, 203-211, 2003.

Levy, Becca, Marin D. Slade and Thomas M. Gill. "Hearing Decline Predicted by Obvious Stereotypes." <u>The Journals of Gerontology Series B; Physiological Series and Social Success</u>, 61, 82-87, 2006.

Lusterbader, Wendy. <u>Counting on Kindness</u>. New York: The Free Press, 1994.

Macy, Joanna. <u>World As Lover</u>. Berkeley, CA: Parallax Press, 1991.

Moslow, Abraham. <u>Motivation and Personality</u>. New York: Harper & Row, 1970.

Montagu, Ashley. <u>Growing Young</u>. Granby, MA: Bergan and Garvey Publications, 1989.

Nagel, Thomas. <u>The Possibility of Altruism</u>. Princeton, NJ: Princeton University Press, 1970.

Neugarten, Bernice. <u>Middle Age and Aging</u>. Chicago and London: The University Press, 1968.

Novak, Michael. <u>The Experience of Nothingness</u>. New York: Harper & Row, 1978.

Peck, Robert. "Psychological Development in the Second Half of Life," in <u>Middle Age and Aging</u>. edited by Bernice Neugarten. Chicago, IL: The University of Chicago Press, 1968.

Pipher, Mary. <u>Another Country: Navigating the Emotional Terrain of Our Elders</u>. New York: Riverhead Books, 1999.

Pollack, George. "The Mourning Process and Creative Organizational Change," <u>Journal of the American Psychoanalytic Association</u>, 25, 3-34, 1977.

Reik, Theodore. <u>Listening with a Third Ear: The Inner Experience of a Psychoanalyst</u>. New York: Farrar, Strauss, and Giroux, 1983.

Rinpoche, Sogyal. <u>The Tibetan Book of Living and Dying</u>. New York: Harper Collins, 1993.

Rosenthal, Hattie. "Psychotherapy for the Dying," in <u>The Interpretation of Death</u>. New York: Jason Aronson, 1973.

Ross, Ernest. <u>The Psychology of Mind and Body Healing</u>. New York: W.W. Norton, 1986.

Rowe, John and Robert Kahn. "Human Aging: Usual and Successful." <u>Science</u>, 61, July, 1987.

Satran, Pamela Redmond. "Small Steps to Boost Your Energy." <u>Ladies Home Journal</u>, 18-22, October, 2005.

Schachter-Shalomi, Zalman. From Aging to Saging. New York: Time Warner, 1995.

Schlossberg, Nancy. <u>Retire Smart, Retire Happy: Finding Your True Path in Life</u>. Washington, D.C.: American Psychological Association, 2004.

Schneidman, Edwin. <u>Voices of Death</u>. New York: Bantam Books.

Schulz, Robert, Carsten Wrosch, and Julie Heckhausen. "The Life Span Theory of Control: Issues and Evidence." in <u>Personal Control in Social and Life Contexts</u>. edited by S.H. Zarit, L.I.I. Pearlin, and K.W. Schaie, New York: Springer, 2003.

Sheehy, Gail. "Life Begins at 60." <u>Parade Magazine</u>, 4-6, December 11, 2005.

Skinner, B.F. "Intellectual Self-Management in Old Age." <u>American Psychologist</u>, 38, 238-244, 1983.

Spark, Muriel. <u>Memento</u>. New York: The Modern Library, 1966.

"The Importance of Doing What's Important to You." Woman's Health Watch III, 6, 1, February, 2001.

Valliant, George. Aging Well. New York: Little, Brown and Company, 2002.

Cort-Van Arsdale, Diane and Phyllis Newman. <u>Transitions: A Woman's Guide to Successful Retirement</u>. New York: Harper and Collins, 1991.

Viorst, Judith. <u>Necessary Losses</u>. New York: Fawcett Gold Medal, 1987.

Wallechensky, David, Irving Wallace and Amy Wallace. The Book of Lists. New York: William Morrow, 1977.

Walsh, Roger and Shauna L. Shapiro. "The Meeting of Meditative Disciplines and Western Philosophy." <u>American Psychologist</u>, 229-236, April, 2006.

Wilson, B.A. and N. Moffat, eds. "Ways to Help Memory." in <u>Clinical Management of Memory</u>, 2nd edition. London: Chapman & Hall, 1992.

Wilson, B.A. <u>Rehabilitation of Memory</u>. New York: Guilford Press, 1987.

Yesavage, J.S. and J. I Sheikh, Z. Friedman, and E. Tante. "Learning Mnemonics: Roles of Aging and Subtle Cognitive Impairment." <u>Psychology of Aging</u>, 5, 133-137, 1989.

Young, Jeffrey E. and Janet S. Klosko. <u>Reinventing Your Life</u>. New York: Plume Books, 1986.

Index

See 1stWorld Books at:

www.1stWorldPublishing.com

See our classic collection at:

www.1stWorldLibrary.org